ELIZABETH YATES

A BIOGRAPHY
AND BIBLIOGRAPHY
OF HER WORKS

BY

Sister Margaret Trudell p.m.

ISBN: 1-4107-0407-6 (e-book)
ISBN: 1-4107-0408-4 (Paperback)

This book is printed on acid free paper.

1stBooks – rev. 03/21/03

TABLE OF CONTENTS

BIBLIOGRAPHY OF WORKS

INTRODUCTION

I first heard the name Elizabeth Yates at a demonstration on Christmas decorating. The lecture took place at the Chandler Memorial Library in Nashua NH. After the demonstration a librarian announced a forthcoming talk by Elizabeth Yates, a New Hampshire author from Peterborough. I cannot recall exactly what she said about her, but I do remember that she spoke of her in such endearing terms that the name entered my brain in a secret compartment where it could be retrieved whenever I needed it. Circumstances prevented me from attending that lecture.

The years went by—maybe seven or eight. Working for a degree in Library Science at Catholic University, I faced the problem of finding a research topic for a major paper required for the degree. I took up a dozen ideas with enthusiasm to begin with, but I soon abandoned them one by one. Four summers passed and my mind was blank and so was that first page of my paper. I then met a fellow student who showed a great deal of enthusiasm about her topic, which was a bio-bibliography of an author. It sounded interesting, besides it seemed easy enough. I thought to myself: "Now, why can't I do something like that with—ELIZABETH YATES" The name just popped out of my head as though it had been lodged on some spring board that had been released by a switch.

Enchanted by this new idea, I began a search in the library to test the substance of this new brain wave. I became very excited as I found articles and books written by Elizabeth Yates. The more I read of her works and about her, the more I became enthusiastic about taking her as a topic for my research. The problem that soon became apparent was "Would I find enough material?" When I presented the topic for approval my director immediately tried to discourage me. "Who is she anyway?" I then explained that she was an author still writing and living in New Hampshire, that she had won the Newbery Medal as well as other awards. Still he did not think this was a feasible topic. He explained that work on a living author could never come to a satisfactory conclusion as there would always be something new coming out year after year. He was right in a way, but I had my heart set on this topic, so I began a little battle to win my case. I had to construct a bibliography for a reference course I was taking at the time, so I decided to use Elizabeth Yates as the subject of my bibliography. Then I could submit the results of a more extensive research. My director accepted this idea. "Great," he said, "we will then decide when we see the results."

Then as a honeybee gets into every flower to seek its sweet nectar, so did I search into every possible book I could think of to find the name: Yates, Elizabeth. The highlight of my research came when I took up *The National Union Catalogue of Manuscript Collections*. It was like finding a map to a gold mine as there was that name again leading me to a collection of papers, manuscripts, letters etc. housed in the special collection room at the Boston University Library.

By the time I was ready to type out my three by five cards, I had arrived at quite a stack. Even then my director did not seem very enthusiastic about my topic. At any rate, I prevailed upon him with the prospect of that special collection which was available to me at Boston University. Also I explained that I hoped to be able to get an interview with the author who resided in Peterborough, which is a short distance from Nashua, NH, where I was stationed at Rivier College. Finally the authorization forms from the office were filled out and signed, giving me the green light to go ahead on my paper. Now I could begin to work in earnest.

Being a full-time librarian, the work progressed at a very slow pace. Little by little I managed to get quite a bit done. I took a few trips to Boston in order to examine the contents of the boxes of the Yates Collection. Mr. Gotlieb, the procurator of the special collection library, was most helpful. My work was so fascinating that the hours spent there seemed like minutes! My little three by fives grew to a mighty stack.

To meet Elizabeth in person for the first time was an exciting experience for me. This happened when she came to give a talk to a group of Education majors on our campus. During the lecture, I was able to examine her as a person and as a speaker. Her whole person radiated deep peace and happiness. A tenderness for all of God's creation was apparent in her way of talking about animals and things. She spoke about her new book, *An Easter Story*. She immediately gained the attention of her audience and held it captive until the end. She gave me the impression of a person who was disciplined but also very humble and accessible. After the lecture I approached her to reveal my project of the bio-bibliography I had undertaken, with the hope of having an interview with her. She seemed to be pleased and promised to see me at some time.

My first visit to Shieling (her home) was in May. She received me warmly into her lovely eighteenth century home. She allowed me to look through a box of papers containing articles and other information which she would eventually forward to Boston University. I had brought along a few of her books which she autographed for me. Nora Unwin, her illustrator of many books, was there also and autographed the books that were illustrated by her, adding to her signature a few flourishes of her delicate art. Before my departure Elizabeth served tea with delicious home made sugar cookies. I was enchanted by that first visit. I was fortunate to have a few other interviews with her as I progressed in my work.

Occasionally, I would send a draft of my paper for her approval. Each time, she would return it promptly with her comments and the corrections she judged necessary. This helped me to finish on time so I could present my paper as a requirement for my degree in Library Science. As soon as the paper was typed and approved, I forwarded a bound copy to Elizabeth Yates as her very own. I received a warm word of gratitude from her immediately.

When I finished my paper in 1970, Elizabeth Yates was still quite active, and has produced many articles and books since then. It was always a bright spot in my day to have a chance meeting with her either at a library meeting or at some other occasion. These last few years when I would meet with her, she would urge me to take up the bio-bibliography so as to bring it up to date. (My director had warned me about taking a living author!)

After giving my old work rest for about thirty years, I have taken it up again. I have added on to the list of books and articles and I have updated the biography. New chapters have been added to highlight the many activities and achievements since 1970.

In 1992 Elizabeth Yates McGreal moved out of her cherished home in Peterborough to take up residence in a retirement community in Concord, NH., called HAVENWOOD - HERITAGE HEIGHTS. Two summers ago I was most fortunate to spend a couple of hours with her in that new location. As ever she received me most graciously. She enjoyed living at Heritage Heights where she could live independently. But in 2001 she moved to Havenwood where she could get the care she needed. She was eagerly awaiting the "big adventure" where she could go to join her dear ones. Two weeks before she died she suffered a stroke. She was taken to the Concord Hospital where she was able to get more care. Then on a Sunday morning, July 29, Elizabeth left us for a better world. She was 95. It was with regret that we learned of her passing away. I, for one, was planning to pay her a visit to have her look over the up-dated version of my bio-bibliography.

When I presented my thesis at Catholic University, she was sixty-four and had written thirty-five books. It was in the field of children's books that she became most famous. Her awards at that time included the Newbery Medal in 1951, the *New York Herald Tribune Children's Spring Book Festival* award in both 1944 and 1950, and the William Allen White Award in 1953. As an adult novelist she has also been successful. Two of her novels, *Nearby* and *Beloved Bondage,* became choices of the People's Book Club. Several have been chosen by the Christian Herald's Family Book Shelf. Two of her biographies, that of Dorothy Canfield Fisher and of Howard Thurman won recognition.

Her writing style is of the highest caliber. The *New York Times* had this to say of the qualities that are typical of her writing: "Her prose style is distinguished even beautiful, in its simplicity, and her deep respect for life shines through every page she writes." 1

The *New York Herald Tribune* highlighted Elizabeth's special talent to make the ordinary things of life come alive with meaning and beauty:

It is a rare talent that makes the small incidents of living so rewarding and sometimes so touched with drama. It is a most unusual talent that takes the reader into the still and sacred places of the heart, and makes him feel at home there. Miss Yates has that talent. 2

Besides being an author of juvenile books, novelist and biographer, Miss Yates is the editor of several books and has written many magazine articles and short stories. Through the years, she became a noted lecturer as well as a public figure in her own state, serving on the State Library Commission and on the Board of Directors of the New Hampshire Association For the Blind; she was also a member of the Committee for Restoration of the Robert Frost Homestead. For a time she was an active member of the Religious Society of Friends and served as Clerk of Monadnock Monthly Meetings.

This paper will present a short biography of the author, highlighting those circumstances in her life that led to her career as a writer. One chapter will study her writing habits and bring to the fore some of the ideas and events that have been the inspiration of some of her books. The same chapter will highlight her speaking career. Following chapters will update her activities pursued in her later years. A list of awards and honors bestowed upon her through the years will be mentioned. The bibliographic section comprises lists of her works arranged by type and in chronological order. For the sake of convenience, I have listed separately the articles she wrote for the *Christian Science Monitor* of Boston. These were articles that depicted the photographs taken by her husband while traveling in Europe.

I wish to express my appreciation for the guidance given me in the preparation of this paper, by Father Bernard Theall of Catholic University of America. To Sister Albina Marie, Head Librarian of Rivier College at the time I completed the first edition, I wish to extend heartfelt thanks for the time allotted me to pursue this research. To Doctor Howard Gotlieb, Chief of Special Collections at Boston University Library, I am grateful for the generous permission to use the material contained in the Yates Collection. To Dr. Paul Lizotte of Rivier College for his encouragement and guidance and to all those who in any way helped me to arrive at the results found herein, I would like to express sincere appreciation.

CHAPTER 1

CHILDHOOD

Born in Buffalo, New York, December 6, 1905, Elizabeth Yates was the daughter of Henry Yates and Mary Duffy. She was next to the youngest of seven children. Her father had an amazingly busy life. He became president of several companies dealing with coal, ice, furnaces, railroads, steamships, banks and hotels. He acquired a farm in Orchard Park, where the family spent the summer months. There he kept two herds of purebred cattle, one of Holstein-Friesan stock and the other of Aberdeen Angus cattle. Her mother, Mary Duffy, was the daughter of Walter Bernard Duffy, who was also a prominent industrialist in the many pursuits he undertook. In that big family Elizabeth was never at a loss for companionship. The Yates family lived a happy combination of country and city life, as the family engaged in farming during the summer months on the father's farm south of Buffalo and spent winters in the city. That Elizabeth became a most remarkably well-balanced person, adapting herself to all the circumstances in her life, is perhaps the result of this happy combination of country-city life in a congenial home atmosphere during her younger years.

Her youth was certainly that of a happy, peaceful child: long summer days spent each year on the farm; long hours of enchanted listening as her mother read to her; long rides on her horse through the country-side, where she loved to be alone in order to think and make up stories of her own. There were plenty of playmates in her brothers and sisters and the numerous pets: dogs, cats, chickens and her treasured horse, called Bluemouse:

I used to go off on my horse for a day at a time, rambling through the countryside, a sandwich in my pocket and the knowledge that any fresh-running stream would give us both drink; but I was never lonely, for there was the horse to talk with and in my head I was writing. On the next rainy day, I would climb the ladder to an unused pigeon loft that was my own secret place and there write down in a series of copy books all that I had been thinking. 1

At an early age Elizabeth knew there was quite a difference between her own picture books and those read by her mother at story time:

My earliest memory of a book is seeing one held lovingly in my mother's hands while she read to us as we sat on the floor before her or curled up on a couch beside her. There were other things that went by the name of books. Some were made of cloth that could be put under a pillow, or chewed, or used in a tug-of-war, and whatever happened to them they came out looking more or less the same. Some were made of paper with stiff covers. A child could look at the pictures and even these, like the rag ones, were given the same treatment as a teddy bear or a doll. This other was different. Mother held it carefully. We leaned over her and looked at it with awe. 2

With Elizabeth, a love for books became second nature. "The house was filled with books, and reading or being read to by my mother was part of our life."3 When she was ten, an older sister made an outline of the reading she thought her younger sister should be doing, which provided a wise guide for many years. Reading became an obsession. She was ingenious in finding secret places where she could read on and on without disturbance. She recalled with a certain delight how she used to hide under a bed and there behind the valence was lost to the world of reality,

> ...vulnerable only to a dust mop or a carpet sweeper. I can remember the safe but wicked joy I felt when I heard my name being called all over the house, especially if my nose was buried in *Oliver Twist* or *At the Back of the North Wind,* which I heard my mother say were too old for me. 4

Being a farm child, Elizabeth had her little chores to do, but she found ways to combine her reading with her job. In some things it worked:

> At home, each one of us had some special task. Mine was to make the butter, several pounds a week for that large family, from the milk and cream always so abundant. In my little dairy, I had a barrel churn that could be worked with one hand. All of Dickens was read one summer as I held a book in one hand and worked the churn with the other. 5

Acquaintance with the Bible, the most cherished book in her life, began at an early age:

> I read the Bible from cover to cover when about 12 - 4 chapters on weekdays, 6 on Sundays taking exactly a year to do it in - because it was my father's wish for all his 7 children, It said something to me then very decidedly and I am glad no one kept it from me until I was old enough to understand it, but it says something very different to

me now. Yet I have often wondered if it was not because of that first acquaintance, impelled as it was by obedience, that it means so much to me now. 6

Christmas vacations were special in the Yates family. The house was decorated with branches of holly and red berries. There was always the marvelous Christmas tree which was burned at the end of the season with a special ritual. Mrs. Yates honored her Irish traditions especially with delicious dishes at the table. Mr. Yates kept to his English customs when he gave each of the household servants a token of appreciation. Most of the presents Elizabeth received were books. She was always eager to get the leisure of enjoying her new books:

I could hardly wait to get into my books but knew it wouldn't be possible until evening. Vacation nights are like Friday nights during school. No homework and bedtime an hour later. I could hardly wait until I could curl up in the big leather chair in the den and read. Soon I'm in another world and the people are as real as the members of my family or my friends at school. 7

Elizabeth was able to experience many cultural opportunities by attending plays at the theater, as well as concerts. Mr. Yates would often bring the group of girls from the club for an outing, most often at the theater. A trip abroad was planned for Betty and Bobby, after Elizabeth's graduation from High School. They spent a few weeks with their parents visiting France and England. It was always a thrill for Elizabeth to see the actual places that she had read about in books: museums, galleries, churches, parks, Notre Dame in Paris. Then in England, more places to see where some of her favorite authors had lived. The castles, the countryside with its rustic dwellings, all was an inspiration to the budding writer.

CHAPTER 2

SCHOOL DAYS

Elizabeth attended the Franklin School in Buffalo, NY, from Kindergarten through high school. This was followed by a year at Oaksmere in Mamaroneck, NY. Before her marriage, she spent some time studying in New York, then again in London.

The Franklin School was blessed with a principal who put a great deal of emphasis on the classics and English Literature. Many prizes were given—most of them books—for accomplishment in different areas. An eager and willing student, Elizabeth built up an excellent library for herself, mainly with prizes gained at school. One of the prizes had been set up for a student who read aloud to an older person for ten minutes a day for the entire school year. As her mother had read to her so often as a child, she, in turn, read to her mother. Seldom, in fact, did the session last the allotted ten minutes, as they most always got carried away by some adventure or episode. [1]

Of her teachers she keeps cherished memories;

I know how much I look back on my teachers now, with a heart almost aching with gratitude for all they gave me, and not a little remorse for all the trouble I gave them…The teachers I think of with most gratitude are the teachers who made books real to me. [2]

Elizabeth loved to write and always got good grades for any of her compositions. As far back as she can remember there was always an urge to write:

I cannot remember a time when there was not in my mind some thought of writing. I can distinctly remember an early spring afternoon in the garden of my childhood home in Buffalo, NY, when I was barely three...I sat under a tree with a picture book, more interested in the shapes of the letters that told the story than in the pictures. With a pencil I tried to copy those letters, thinking in some oddly infantine way that if I did so I would be writing a book. Our nurse discovered what I was doing, and to my surprise, reprimanded me for marking up the pages of my 'pretty book'. 3

Possessed with a lively imagination while still a child, Betty was always making up stories of her own. Each evening brought a story read to her by mother or father. When the book was closed, the story went on in her head:

We would listen with eager attention, following the adventure or fascinated by the words. It always ended too soon, yet each of us knew that Mother had only commenced something that would go on and on. Our minds were filled with pictures quiet with things to think about. Climbing into bed, I felt almost eager for the moment when the light would be put out and the room would slide into darkness, for then I could go on with the story in my own way, in my own `mind. 4

It was during her school days that Elizabeth began to show her leadership qualities. The war affected her as well as her friends. She helped to organize a club called "Just Us Girls". With much effort they raised money by spending many hours making items for a bazaar. The money they made was sent to help out victims of the war, especially children.

The war brought about tragedies that touched the lives of everyone. It was during the war that she became aware of the awesome meaning of death. One of her school teachers was a victim of the influenza epidemic. It was the first time she saw a dead person when she attended the funeral with her mother. The death of Jean's brother Alan, who was killed while on military duty in France, hit her even harder. Jean was her best friend, so her big brother meant much to both of them.

Her first great thrill in writing came in her last year at school. She had written an essay on Browning. The paper was returned to her with a large "A" appended with the short remark: "delightful paper to read". In her heart this success only confirmed her desire to go on writing and perhaps make it her life work:

The mark meant only that my facts were correct, that most of my commas were in the right places, and that no words were mis-spelled; but that my work had been "a delight to read"—that was something to feel excited about! I had a feeling that for once words had bent to my desire. I glimpsed something then that I was to see ever more clearly—that the writer only commences; it is the reader who completes. I stood at the base of the long mountain before me. I could take a deep breath for the climb ahead. 5

When the results of the College Board Examinations came in at the end of her senior year in High School, Elizabeth had failed in Algebra and Geometry. She could not go to college unless she worked trying to pass the tests again. It was decided that college was not for her. Her parents decided to enter her at Oaksmere in Mamaroneck, N Y, for a year at boarding school. With another year of education they thought she would be better prepared for life. They were hoping that Elizabeth would give up the thought of becoming a writer and were looking forward to presenting her to the elite society of Buffalo. Before going to boarding school she had a good talk with her father and made a pact with him, that if she attended the school for a year she would then be free to pursue her wish to be on her own the following year. Mr. Yates agreed and they both shook hands over it.

During the year she spent at Oaksmere, she would travel every Friday morning into New York City to meet with Miss Russell who had been hired to help her to improve her writing skills. These lessons brought her closer to the goal she was striving for. Miss Russell sent one of her poems to the *Newark Evening News.* What a surprise for Elizabeth when she came in the next week to find that one of her poems had found its way to publication. Elizabeth was on cloud nine. Then one day as she came to the dear lady's door, a note on the door revealed that Miss Russell had passed on to another world. Again she felt the undeniable void caused by death.

After the year at Oaksmere, Elizabeth applied for a job at a summer camp. There she taught riding and was requested to write in the weekly paper. The summer went by like a breeze as she enjoyed her job to the fullest. Her parents were dismayed that she insisted on being on her own in New York. They tried to discourage her, but to no avail. Their hope was to present her as a debutante to the society of Buffalo, but that was not what Elizabeth desired. Her tastes were plain and simple. High Society was not for her. She was finally allowed to leave for the big city where writing opportunities would be more plentiful.

In New York she shared an apartment with Martha, one of her classmates from Buffalo who also wanted to find her own way as an artist. During her stay there, she held a variety of jobs, doing anything worthwhile that came along. At one time, she worked as a comparison shopper for R.H. Macy. Of that job she says: "It was fascinating, hard work and fun."6 Most of her evenings were spent writing, as she took any opportunity to write an article or a review for some magazine or newspaper. She was scrupulous in following the advice that Miss Russell gave her to write something everyday, no matter what. Thus began the long apprenticeship of ten years. It was only by keeping at it that she would be able to master the words sufficiently to become a writer by profession.

CHAPTER 3

MARRIED LIFE

Elizabeth met William McGreal at a party in New York. He was immediately attracted to this shy but intelligent girl. This is how he described that first meeting:

Behind her slightly shy brown eyes there was a seriousness not wholly concealed by a frequent twinkle. 'Small talk' was not her forte. When she spoke, it was of things she felt. She was forth-right. I liked her. We made a date. The following Saturday found us atop Timp, one of the so-called peaks in the Hudson Highlands. Our campfire had died down to embers. Elizabeth closed the little worn volume she had brought in her knapsack and leaned back against the ledge. After a moment she said, "That's good writing. Someday I too, shall write something good." I felt no need to respond. We sat for a long time looking across the foothills...It was no doubt during that happy day on Timp that I first saw many qualities of the real person—a love of mankind and nature; a zest for the outdoors and high places; a courage and stamina; a striving and searching.1

As William's work took him to London, the romance continued in correspondence and messages sent back and forth across the Atlantic. One day a special cablegram came with the summons that she should join him to get married in London. Elizabeth eagerly packed her belongings and joined him there, to become his bride in 1929. Ten years of happy living followed. Vacations took them mountain-climbing in Switzerland, on a pack horse trip in Iceland, and as tourists to many of the countries of Europe. During her stay in London or on her travels in Europe, Elizabeth continued to write. An occasional short story or a poem got into print, as well as many reviews and articles on travel. These were published in the *Christian Science Monitor* of Boston. In the course of this period in London she also wrote a few plays for school children. Her first book, *High Holiday*, a story of two English children spending a summer vacation mountain-climbing in Switzerland, was accepted by the first publisher it was sent to. While in London, she continued to indulge in the favorite pastime of her youth, spending many hours reading in the British Museum.

Because of William's failing eyesight, after ten years in London, the McGreals decided to settle down to a more quiet life. Returning to the United States, they decided that they wanted to live on a farm, After an extensive search, they found a small farmhouse which suited their taste, near the town of Peterborough, New Hampshire. A complete renovation of the house brought about interesting discoveries. Sturdy fireplaces which had been boarded up were restored and put to good use. Stencil designs on the walls of one room, done by a nineteenth-century journeyman painter, were discovered by steaming off several layers of wall paper. These were carefully restored and this latter discovery became the inspiration of one of Elizabeth's prize-winning books: *Patterns on the Wall.* 2

The McGreals settled down to country living. A garden was plowed and cultivated, and a flock of hens purchased. Many walks were taken on their sixty-seven acres, half of which were wooded.

It was during that first winter that William lost his eyesight, following an operation which the doctors had hoped would be successful. For one terrible moment the truth almost crushed Elizabeth:

It was not until I was driving back to the country that the full import of what he (the doctor) had said got through me. Then resentment and bitterness shook me like hurricane winds. I would not, could not, believe what had happened to Bill. I stopped the car for I could not see to drive. I beat my hands on the steering wheel. Images raced through my mind: places where we had lived, mountains we had climbed. Each one was torture, for all I could think was that Bill would not see them again. Then I thought of Bill and the depths he must have reached during his weeks alone in the hospital. 3

Elizabeth was not one to give up in despair. The thought of her husband who would need her more than ever, who depended on her guiding hand to go through life, helped to rally her spirits. She set about with a determination to make life as easy as she could for him. Never again did she give in to despair. Her husband later wrote these words of praise:

When confronted by a challenge or faced by a danger she is at her best. Her resourcefulness and courage filled a need more than once when we were climbing in Switzerland or on a pack trip in Iceland. About eight years ago, this steadiness of spirit had to meet a different kind of crisis when I lost my sight. Not once did Elizabeth falter. There was no tragedy, no defeat. Though the adjustment seemed so very slow at first, I gained hope and confidence as I felt her closer companionship, her strong hand in mine and her unconquerable spirit. 4

Taking upon herself chores that had been done by her husband, she endeavored to make his life as full as it had ever been. She found many ways to make her husband's life more bearable, helping him to find a new road to independence. Above all she filled his life with her loving and compassionate companionship. Before long, William found his way around and gradually took on tasks he had temporarily given up:

Bill had always liked to work out problems, mathematical ones especially. Blindness was an intriguing problem, and as he found the solution to some of its difficult aspects he began to handle himself with an ease that looked like emancipation from blindness. 5

He studied and mastered Braille, and his life began to reach out to others, as he was offered a job which he accepted at Perkins Institute for the Blind. Then he became the first Executive Director of the New Hampshire Association For The Blind, a post he kept from 1947-1956. He continued in the Association as first vice president of the Board of Directors. In 1963, William McGreal died of a heart attack.

After having lived such a loving, intimate relationship with Bill, Elizabeth had to face the reality that he would no longer be there to share her life. Turning to her art of writing again, she produced: *Up the Golden Stair.* The following is an excerpt found in the Forward of the book:

—I was called upon to put my long-held thoughts to the test—not of words on paper but in the living of one day after another without the near presence of the one with whom I had shared everything that was life for more than thirty-four years: joy and sorrow, success and despair, high-hearted delight, soul-sounding trials. 6

CHAPTER 4

CIVIC LIFE AND INTERESTS

Keeping a very tight schedule, and reserving morning hours for writing, Elizabeth spent the rest of the day in a number of practical occupations. The care of her beautiful home called Shieling, hours of reading alone or with others, walks in the countryside accompanied by her dog were the usual relaxations from the long hours of writing. When the weather was favorable, she worked in a well-kept garden. Needlepoint, rug hooking and knitting kept her hands busy while in the company of friends or while listening to the radio. She delighted in receiving visitors, for whom she often turned out a delicious meal at a rather short notice.

CONTRIBUTIONS TO LIBRARIES

Her contribution to the Peterborough Public Library as an active trustee was invaluable. Attending to the general appearance of the library, both inside and out, became a self-imposed task. Ann Geisel, former librarian said of her: "Elizabeth was one of the most vital people I know. She was a powerhouse as a trustee, yet so unassuming; a sweetheart who was always thinking of how other people would feel. She was always generous and so 'young - thinking'…"All the children around here knew her. She led the story Hour at the Library for years. Youngsters were constantly inspired by her and her books." [1]

When a new room was added to the Peterborough library, many wanted it to be called the Elizabeth Yates Room, but when Elizabeth heard of this she immediately proposed that it should be called the Elizabeth Room. At once she initiated the idea of inviting all the Elizabeths to contribute to the room. There was such a generous response from so many of the Elizabeths reached, that a total of $250,000 was raised from large checks as well as pennies from Piggy Banks.

At one time she even consented to be part of a special telephone - television hook-up, answering questions from children in Columbia, Missouri. In fact, her interest in libraries reached beyond her own small town. She served on many library committees on a state-wide level. In 1962 she was the chairman of the National Library Week Program in New Hampshire. In 1965, Governor King appointed her a member of the State Library Commission, a post she held until 1978.

Elizabeth was instrumental in forming the Friends of the Peterborough Library. She also organized a reading group, whose members remained in contact with her after she left for Concord. They would inform her of the books they were reading and she was always faithful in responding.

Elizabeth was generous with her time and in other ways, as this 1984 excerpt from the *NH State Library Biennial Report* describes:

Another successful project was the updating of *Good Reading for Youth,* published by the State Library in 1963. The updated work, entitled, *Witch in the Woods,* was partially funded by Elizabeth Yates McGreal and distributed to all school and public libraries. The remaining 1,000 copies were sold for a small fee to anyone desiring a copy. 2

Again in 1989 Mrs. McGreal made a most appropriate contribution to small libraries in New Hampshire:

Libraries serving populations of under 2,000 received a copy of *The Road Taken: The New Hampshire Library Association, 1889-1989.* The thoughtful donation of this excellent history is testimony to her caring and concern for the state's smallest libraries. Her unselfish acts will be long remembered by the library community and the people of New Hampshire. Mrs. McGreal has our heartfelt and warmest thanks.3

For a period of twelve years, before the Peterborough Library took on the regular sessions of story-telling it now has, Elizabeth would gather the children of the neighborhood, in her own home, to entertain them with her special art of story-telling. She spent many hours as a volunteer in nursing homes and hospitals, most of the time reading to the patients and seeing to their needs. They always looked forward to her visits. She was such a vibrant person that she made the atmosphere delightful whenever she showed up.

ELIZABETH YATES AS TEACHER

It never occurred to Elizabeth that she had the makings of a teacher. But she was ever ready to encourage aspiring writers and would freely give young writers advice to improve their work. She was invited by the University of New Hampshire to take part in a Writer's Conference that would be given there. That first experience was an enjoyable success and so she accepted to partake of many others, not only in New Hampshire but in other states where Writers' Conferences were given.

Beverly Gordon was one writer who was helped by Elizabeth Yates:

"I always had a quiet desire to write," Gordon says, but she hadn't considered professional writing a possibility until she met McGreal about ten years ago. McGreal had called her after seeing the family history Gordon had written. "I think you can be a writer," Gordon remembers McGreal saying. "Her confidence in me was very motivating, she encouraged me to start with small things then to a step up. 4

This encouragement resulted in helping Beverly Gordon to become a published writer. Her first book, *The First Year Alone,* was published in 1986.

White Pines College, a fairly new college located in Chester, NH, also benefited from the author's interest. She became a trustee and even initiated a resident writer's program at the college.

CONSERVATIONIST

One of Elizabeth Yates' greatest concerns was conservation of the land. Her book, *The Road through Sandwich Notch* is the telling of the nine mile walk back and forth that Elizabeth took with her dog, Sir Gibbie. In the book she points out several historic places and gives reasons why this road should be preserved. The book helped to raise support for saving the area from developers, and Sandwich Notch became part of the White Mountains National Forest.

Again she donated her own land, which consisted of 47 acres of wooded land, to the State of New Hampshire. This has been called Shieling Forest, under the care of the Division of Forests and Lands for the State of N.H. It is a learning center for farmers with wooded lots. Elizabeth also gave an endowment which will permit the state to upkeep the Forest for educational purposes.

INVOLVEMENT WITH THE NEW HAMPSHIRE
ASSOCIATION FOR THE BLIND

Elizabeth became involved in the Association when her husband Bill became blind and when he took on the duties of first executive director in 1947. She was an active supporter of her husband's duties, helping him in any way she could. William McGreal, being a businessman, took his job seriously. He established the Association services statewide, traveling to the homes of the blind and visually impaired. He also left the Association on a firm financial footing, by initiating fund-raising activities to support the services given throughout the state. A program of mailings started in 1948 continues to support the Association to this day.

In 1965 Elizabeth came on the Board and served until 1988. She was president from 1977-1984. When she retired from service she was elected the first Director Emeritus until her death in 2001. When Mr. Gale Stickler was asked to describe Elizabeth Yates as president, he replied:

I never think of her as president. I think of her as a person, a bright, articulate person with vision for the future. As a leader, Elizabeth allowed lots of interchange of ideas. She was always interested in the opinions of others. I don't believe Elizabeth ever killed an idea in her life."5

Stickler describes how he and Elizabeth Yates stood one day in the midst of the chaos of renovating the old parochial school on Walker Street into the modern center: "Elizabeth and I looked down into the rubble of the gutted building. I only saw headaches, frustrations, problems. Elizabeth said, "What a tremendous facility we shall have soon for doing our work." 6

During her mandate as president, a major fund campaign was begun to raise a million dollars. Also an old school building was purchased and renovated. In June of 1985 the building was dedicated and called the McGREAL SIGHT CENTER, to honor William and Elizabeth McGreal. The keynote address was given by Charles D. Baker, Under Secretary of the United States Department of Health and Human Services. Walter Peterson, president of Franklin Pierce College, spoke of the McGreals with great admiration:

"William McGreal traveled throughout this state…to bring the message to the blind and visually impaired that they could achieve their goals of self-care and self-esteem. Bill was a man of great dedication who worked tirelessly and courageously. A torch was passed when Bill died in 1963 and Elizabeth assumed a place on the Association's board. she is a vital, giving person, has worked in every way possible to improve her community, her state, and the lot of others. Throughout her personal life, she's been an example of the finest personal qualities, of strong personal faith…a concern and commitment to better the lives of others…"[7]

Mr. Peterson then offered Mrs. McGreal a dozen of roses. Elizabeth must have been touched by this gesture as Bill always gave her roses on their wedding anniversary, Nov. 6th. In her response on this memorable day Elizabeth explained the meaning of the McGreal name:

"On this splendid occasion I would like to share with you a brief story about the name 'McGreal', in the middle ages surnames related to a person's occupation, adventures or exploits. There were many who were on the quest for the holy grail. Grail, Greal, Grill, many spellings became attached to them, and also, in time, the addition of Mc and Mac. They were known as those who had gone on a difficult pilgrimage. "Whatever the 'grail' might be or have been - a chalice or dish - it was a symbol of light. I feel, with this building dedicated today as the McGREAL SIGHT CENTER, that the quest is continuing…because those of the staff who serve here with such devotion and dedication, and those clients who come here in such need, are coming to a place that is a symbol of light."[8]

A partial renewal of the school building was done and dedicated in 1984. As the Association developed, all the building was refurbished and on September 17, 1998, another dedication took place in a ribbon cutting ceremony. Mrs. McGreal was there and gave a few inspiring words. Her opening lines were: "With you I share the joy of this day that marks another onward step in the reach and achievement of the New Hampshire Association for the Blind."9

After the renovations in 1985 the Center was able to take in more activities and had space for the agency's social workers and rehabilitation specialists. It could provide for low vision programs and group activities, volunteer programs and a small library of large print books:

The association helps visually impaired individuals to overcome the trauma of losing eye-sight, teaches safe and independent travel methods, instructs in the skills of daily living, and offers cultural leadership and support programs. The low vision clinic evaluates and prescribes aids such as high powered telescopes, biotic lenses, even lighting, to make the best use of limited eyesight. The homecraft program teaches skills providing therapeutic and constructive use of leisure time, and through the Lamplighter Shop, an opportunity for blind craftsmen to earn an income...Most services are provided in the community. A fully-equipped mobile van carries the low vision program to local communities and a branch office in Berlin serves the North Country.10

The financial condition of the Association is assured by the establishment of the William and Elizabeth Yates McGreal Society. The members commit some of their estate to benefit the Center. Mrs. McGreal has specified "that her Estate will forward the proceeds of her many books to help fund the Association's specialized service programs"11

Boredom and selfishness were unknown to Elizabeth Yates. Her husband once said of her: "Usefulness seems to be the yardstick of her philosophy beginning at home, then community, and through her writing broadening into an ever wider field."12

CHAPTER 5

FRIEND AND ILLUSTRATOR
NORA UNWIN

Nora Unwin was born in Tolworth, Surrey a few miles outside of London, from a long line of printers and publishers. At an early age she learned to carve wood blocks. Her artistic talent became apparent as a young child. She studied art under Leon Underwood, then after two years went on to study at the Kingston School of Art. She then won a scholarship to the Royal College of Art in London, becoming an accomplished artist, especially in the field of wood blocking. Many of her prints have found their way in prominent museums such as the British Museum, The Library of Congress, Boston Public Library and others. She was asked to give exhibits of her prints in Art Galleries all over America as well as in Europe. One English newspaper, the *Surrey Advertiser,* reviewed her work and wrote:

"Miss Unwin is considered one of the World's finest living wood engravers."[1]

Elizabeth and Bill McGreal first met Nora in London when her twin sister Nancy introduced her to them. This meeting with the McGreals developed into a lifelong friendship. The writer and the artist soon joined their talents to produce books with illustrations that would capture the minds and hearts of thousands of eager juvenile readers. Thus began a partnership that lasted to the end of Nora's life.

When the McGreals left England, Nora took them to the ship which would bring them to the United States. She had become so close to them that the separation was wrenching but the McGreals invited her to visit them as soon as she could come. Once Elizabeth and Bill were settled in their home on the outskirts of Peterborough NH, the illustrator and the writer exchanged letters, manuscripts and illustrations. Because of war conditions in England, artists there had difficulty finding enough work to support themselves. Nora's dream was to go to America, where she could find more openings for her work. Her friends kept inviting her, but when she applied for the necessary papers to exit from England, she ran into one snag after another. Finally, with the help of Ambassador Winant, former governor of New Hampshire, Nora was able to land safely April 18, 1946, at La Guardia airport where Elizabeth met her with open arms. New England was a whole new revelation to the artist and she instantly fell in love with the countryside. This is how she described her first impressions of New England:

> Oh, that drive was heavenly. These great glorious wide roads. The New English countryside has won my heart completely. There is something so gracious, genial, and stately about these white wooden houses and tinted shutters. The little white churches with pointed spires, the tall, fan-shaped elm trees and green grass surrounds the houses, which are built at all angles to each other, giving such an individuality to each. 2

Then as the car approached Shieling, she recognized it because she had seen photographs that had been sent to her. She recalled the gracious welcome she received from Bill and Elizabeth:

The house is everything that one would expect of Elizabeth, combining comfort, order, daintiness, thoughtfulness and beauty...Bill came out to greet us and gave me such a welcome, what a pet he is. I don't think Elizabeth has changed a scrap in seven years. Bill is absolutely fine. It is grand the way he manages and can do a lot, in spite of his handicap, and his cheery good humor is as jolly as ever. The first thing I did was to have a hot bath up to my neck. Then a delicious supper over the fire with a real English pot of tea! I slept around the clock. Elizabeth brought me a breakfast tray with a vase of three daffodils that had just bloomed. 3

Nora was given a small room which served as her bedroom and studio. Both the writer and the artist spent mornings at their own specific work, Elizabeth writing and Nora preparing illustrations. Now that Nora was in the country and available, she received many orders from various publishers, and her fine work came to be known. As she became familiar with the marvels of New England, she became positive that she had done the right thing by coming to America. Her bubbly personality added a special touch to Shieling. She was included in all their doings. In the book, *The Lighted Heart,* she is called Mary. There we can appreciate how Elizabeth and Bill shared their lives with her. She was so very useful to Bill when Elizabeth had to be absent for conferences or talks. Though she was not a cook, she took upon herself to serve Sunday morning breakfast, always serving corn bread and scrambled eggs with fruit of the season.

The small room soon became too cluttered for a decent working area, so when Nora was gone to England for a visit, the McGreals had the old carriage shed remodeled into a comfortable apartment with a spacious studio and living quarters as well. Needless to say Nora was overcome with joy and gratitude upon her return to Shieling. She enjoyed the new studio for a few years, but she then began to feel that she wanted a change. She wanted to explore Boston, so she took up residence in Wellesley near Boston. She also did some teaching at Tenacres school. She then went for some time to Mexico. After four years away she came back to Shieling. Bill and Elizabeth offered to build her a better dwelling. So Pine Apple Cottage came into being. It had everything an artist could desire as a working area and pleasant living quarters to boot. Elizabeth and Nora joined their efforts in producing 26 books. There existed a close and deep friendship between them. Elizabeth portrayed her friend in simple but loving terms:

She is slim and very trim in dress and appearance. She has a merry nature, laughing easily with others or at herself, or alone if she has good reason. Her own taskmaster, she can give herself guerdons when due, mindful always of the words of a teacher at her college, 'Please yourself or you please no one.'…She has great tenderness with animals. She meets children on an equal footing that makes them love her and pose readily for her. Her capacity to enjoy life either alone when absorbing nature for her work or with others is immense. Nora Unwin is a radiant, outpouring person, and it is fortunate for the world that she has the medium of art through which the richness of her being can reach far. 4

Jennifer DuBois, an interviewer, gave her impressions of the great friendship between Nora and Elizabeth. Each one admired the "qualities in the other that she herself lacked. Elizabeth was down-to-earth and practical; Nora was ethereal. Elizabeth didn't have that fairy-tale quality; Nora was a fairy-tale person. She was imaginative, sparkling. Nora didn't worry about worldly things; she thought about life, art and nature."5

Nora had jotted in a notebook: "Elizabeth brings to mind a tall pine tree, erect, strong, fresh and good, firmly rooted in the solid earth." There follows an effusive tribute to her courage, her zest for life, her self-discipline, her sense of service to others, and "a quiet assurance that inspires the love and confidence of the people, children and animals around her." She concluded with a poem called "Someone I Know"

> Tall and straight and rooted deep
> In earth and stones, a pine will keep
>   its tryst in any weather;
> So too is she, as the evergreen tree.
> Holding, she grows in adversity—
>   the greater the challenge, the better.
>
> As pine is true to its resinous self,
> Bears and sheds its growth and its wealth,
>   shelters and gives its shadow,
> Creates a beauty where it stands
> In sun or rain, diagrams
>   its shape in sunny hollow.
>
> So she stands, and grows, and gives,
> Partaking of beauty where she lives
>   to share in doubled measure
> As pine speaks, through sweet-throated birds,
> She listens, and in cadenced words
>   sends forth her mind's deep treasure. 6

On May first of 1976 Nora suffered a first stroke followed by a few others. Each time she rallied and always kept her sunny disposition. There came a time when she could not paint any longer. She used markers and produced a few interesting pieces. Students and friends helped her through these trying times. The news that Nancy., her twin, had died was a blow to her. There came a time when she felt she could no longer produce. She felt she had done all she could do. She became more frail, but to the end the smile was always there. "She was a blithe and bonny spirit whose joy never flagged."[7]

On January 5, 1982, Nora Spicier Unwin died.[8]

CHAPTER 6

ELIZABETH YATES, WRITER

In the peace and quiet of "Shieling," every morning, Elizabeth Yates was perched in a small but cozy loft, facing the beauty of the surrounding mountains. Except for a table, a chair, and a Franklin stove, there was nothing there that could be a distraction. With the faithful companionship of her dog, mornings were spent filling pages and pages which eventually would become a book. To these pages she brought the ideals and values that inspired her life.

Inspirations came to her at the most unexpected moments. These ideas she kept to herself, letting her imagination work its own magic web:

A story is only as good as the idea prompting it and the idea holds within it all possibilities. The idea is the story as, in a manner of speaking, the acorn is the oak...If cherished (the idea), the words will grow from it. This is, perhaps, the artist's secret. He has very little to do with his work for once the idea is grasped it will do it for him.1

Curiosity takes over at times, leading to extensive research for a biography or some other work of information. *Amos Fortune, Free Man,* was begun at a grave site in Jaffrey, New Hampshire, which she happened to visit one lovely summer evening. Intrigued by the epitaph on the tombstone, she became curious. It read as follows:

31

Sacred to the memory of Amos Fortune who was born free in Africa, a slave in America, he purchased liberty, professed Christianity, lived reputably and died hopefully, November 17, 1801. Aet. 912

Her research in town papers and libraries resulted in the beautiful story which won wide acclaim and the Newbery Medal.

On another occasion, it took only a short caption in the *New York times* to stimulate her imagination to fresh efforts. The caption and article read:

ENGLISH TOWN GREETS HERONS

Chilham, England, Feb. 14 (UPI) - - It is a happy St Valentine's Day today for Chilham. The herons came back on time to keep their 1,000- year-old date. According to local legend, their arrival on or before St Valentine's Day means well and good for the village during the year.3

From these words was born *The Next Fine Day,* a charming story of a widow and her son, linked delicately with the flight of the herons.

Love for animals and farm life can be found in *Mountain Born, A Place for Peter,* and *Is there a Doctor in the Barn?* A special love for horses gave rise to *Hue and Cry* and *Brave Interval.* Mountain climbing, one of her favorite sports, was the background for her first book, *High Holiday.*

Her love for dogs was the inspiration of at least three of her books. When she became aware of a special training for dogs at the University of Michigan Medical Center, she made it a point to investigate and went to

Michigan to see for herself. She then witnessed how the dogs were able to do what people could not do for emotionally disturbed children. So then on her return to her writing quarters, *Skeezer, Dog with a Mission* was born. NBC made a film out of this fascinating story of Skeezer. Likewise, the book *Sound Friendships, The Story of Willa and her Hearing Ear Dog,* was also based on a training program geared to assist the deaf and the severely hearing impaired. These dogs are trained to respond to sounds so they can alert a deaf person when a need arises. Their training is similar to that of seeing eye dogs. *The Seventh One* is a story of dogs. Elizabeth brings into this book all the dogs that have enriched her life through the years.

Something that had happened during the pioneer days of Northern New Hampshire was brought to her attention. A little child of three had been lost in the woods for three days. There seemed to be no hope of finding her alive, but a miracle came to the rescue and the child was found, much to the relief of her parents. Elizabeth was touched to write *Sarah Whitcher's Story*. Before writing the story, she went to visit the vicinity where this marvelous event took place.

The Road through Sandwich Notch was prompted by Elizabeth's conservation ideals. She heard that developers were on the verge of taking this historic road. She walked the nine mile road back and forth with her dog Sir Gibbie and then wrote the book that helped to save the Notch, which became part of the White Mountains National Forest.

Elizabeth Yates was a woman of prayer and of deep personal faith. This stamp of faith can be found in all of her books. *Your Prayers and Mine* is a compilation of beautiful short prayers lovingly culled through the years. *Children of the Bible, An Easter Story, Up the Golden Stair,* and *The Lighted Heart* are particularly characterized by a loving and living faith.

Critiques and reviews of Elizabeth Yates' books are in general most favorable. Young and old enjoy reading her books, as her work is characterized by a splendid versatility.

This is an unusual quality in the work of any writer and in that of Elizabeth Yates the material for each age level is beautifully written and plot is carefully delineated. These books are not time wasters. They are profound mirrors of the best kinds of human experience with which thoughtful and eager young people are vitally concerned.4

Although we live in an age of strife and bewilderment, one that has engendered authors whose works are full of pessimism and dismal fear, Elizabeth Yates' work is characterized by a placid optimism which brings hope to those who read her books. Marie Cimino has very accurately summed up these qualities:

A rare thing at all times and perhaps rarer today is the pervasive atmosphere of serenity, gentleness, and idealism that suffuses the entire work of Elizabeth Yates. Even in the preoccupations which she shares with many other writers of this time, as in her concern for the downtrodden and her efforts to combat prejudice, she never succumbs to the infection of the prevailing bitterness and realistic pessimism. Her intense love of nature and all creatures and her warm faith in the omnipresence of nobility, even in the smallest things, lull the skepticism of the reader and coax him into at least a temporary acceptance of her world.5

ELIZABETH YATES, SPEAKER

From early childhood, a desire to write had always been in Elizabeth Yates. But the thought of becoming a speaker had never troubled her, until invitations came, asking for a lecture or a talk. She knew she must accept, for public speaking, she felt, was part and parcel of a writer's career. Overcoming an innate shyness, she met this new challenge in all earnestness. She read books on public speaking, jotting down, for further assimilation notes which she thought were most pertinent. Some of these can be found in her notebook on speeches. Here are a few:

Be informal, gay, confidential, - - Enjoy the telling and they will the listening. - - Talk to - - not at - - your audience. You and your audience must feel a message. Eat sparingly as a saint. - - Feel the charm of language.6

Every talk was prepared with meticulous care, the content enforced by extensive research, the text written out in flawless prose and rehearsed with determined persistence. No need to be timid or uneasy, as she realized with Robinson that "Fear is the result of ignorance and uncertainty." 7 From the Bible, she drew inspiration from Isaiah: "Lift up your voice. Be not afraid."8 Then from Chronicles: "He did with all his heart and prospered."9

Assisted by her husband, she became an excellent speaker. When Mildred Mckay, state librarian, complimented her as being the best author-speaker she had ever heard, Elizabeth Yates replied that it was thanks to her husband. "If you are going to lecture, do it well," he had said, then appointed himself her private tutor and critic.10

She has given lectures on many subjects: from a talk on Iceland to an informal chat on how a book came into being. Always she managed to captivate her audience. Many newspaper clippings found in the Elizabeth Yates Collection give flattering reports of her talks:

> A plainly dressed but completely charming Elizabeth Yates delighted her audience at the Writers' Conference Thursday night with an unaffected simplicity that held it spellbound, and changed its moods from laughter to tears.11

Occasionally, she spoke at graduations or at banquets. Teachers, librarians and clubs who invited her to speak drew much benefit from her experience and were invariably delighted. When she received an honorary degree at Rivier College, she brought up the quest she went through to find a bobby pin. It amused the audience.

Starting in 1948, she became a staff member at many Writers' Conferences. These brought her to the Universities of New Hampshire, Colorado, Indiana, Connecticut, Minnesota. For twelve years, she was on the staff for the Christian Writers and Editors' Conferences at Green Lake, Wisconsin. In 1964, she gave a series of lectures as "Writer in Residence" at Aurora College, Aurora, Illinois.

I had the opportunity to hear Miss Yates speak on several occasions. I was able to judge for myself the reaction her talks had on those who were there. The perfect diction, the dignified poise, the intimacy with which she spoke soon had her entire audience at perfect attention. There was that unmistakable animation and interest that a good speaker knows how to stimulate. One could have listened to her for hours. After the lecture, she was available for anyone who wanted to speak with her. To those who sought her, she was amiable and obliging, answering every question at length and in a sympathetic way.

CHAPTER 7

SHIELING FOREST

When the McGreals moved into their renovated farm house in 1941, they gave it the name SHIELING which is the Scottish name meaning shelter. In Scotland, the name is given to a small hut protecting shepherds from the weather.

With the house, 67 acres of land became the property of the McGreals. Most of it was wooded with a brook running through it. They rented the fields to farmers in need of extra pastures. A garden plot furnished their table with an abundance of vegetables, and a flock of hens supplied them with plenty of eggs. They also derived some income from the lumber taken from the land by selected cutting and there was always a good supply of firewood.

After Bill's death in 1963 and the passing of the years, Elizabeth wanted to make the land useful to others. One of her cherished dreams was to create a small colony of retired persons. The plan comprised the building of small cottages surrounding her own home, where life could be enjoyed and shared. After working out the plan and negotiating with contractors, it soon became apparent that it was not feasible; because of inflation, the cost of building had become prohibitive, and the idea was set aside. Then another possibility began to develop. Could the land be used as a conservation area? This idea was appealing as Elizabeth had always been a conservationist. Most of her books reflect her love of nature, animals, birds and all of God's Creation. Her thoughts turned to saving Shieling that others might enjoy it as she and her husband had through the years. She therefore approached Mr. Theodore Natti, Director of the Division of Forests and Lands for the State of New Hampshire. After a long period of planning and negotiations, the property now known as Shieling Forest, was officially turned over to the State of New Hampshire in 1979.

J.B. Cullen, Chief, Forest Information on Planning with The Division of Forests and Lands, explained that "Several people have donated their land and buildings to the state. The State is beginning to look at these donations more closely because of the need for a solid financial foundation to insure the long term commitments. Shieling Forest was given an endowment and this makes our program and maintenance possible." Mr. Cullen went on to explain that "Shieling Forest is special because 90,000 land owners in New Hampshire own approximately 80% of all the land. The average size land holding in New Hampshire is 45 acres. Shieling Forest is 47 acres. That gives us an opportunity to demonstrate what can be done on an average size wood lot in New Hampshire."

The program at Shieling Forest is set up to deliver pertinent information, expand knowledge, and motivate small wood lot owners to manage their trees and their forests. At Shieling Forest, there is a Forestry Learning center where Foresters explain the theory and the forest itself provides the demonstration. "Here we will set up demonstrations that will show people how forest management can be accomplished on small wood lots," explained Mr. Cullen. During the summer months a series of programs are offered to small wood lot owners. In addition to educating small wood lot owners, the Shieling Forest program lists other objectives in its Annual Report "to provide forestry information to the public, and develop the forest resources and property for convenient public access and use:" Every year, on Arbor Day or during Conservation Week, school children come to participate in a special program organized by the foresters.

Since Shieling Forest has been under the control of the state, much work has been done to make the property accessible to the general public. The foresters have developed a splendid network of trails with attractive carved signs at each intersection. There are Trail Guides available in the parking lot which give pertinent information about trees and other points of interest along the way.

My own personal experience of Shieling Forest began a nippy November day when I went to explore the area with a friend who is a nature photographer. Traveling north along Old Street Road and crossing Sand Hill Road, we saw the sign for Shieling Forest. In the parking lot, we consulted the large weatherproof map where all the trails are clearly indicated. Below the map, the trail guides could be found. Following the guide I could reach the points of interest: a white mulberry tree, Dunbar Brook, a maple sugar house, two extremely large boulders, a granite quarry, The Hadley Brickyard.

The trails are open during daylight hours for hiking, cross-country skiing, snow-shoeing or just for plain relaxing. Nature lovers will find their delight in the beauty of this forest. Even in November, I discovered princess pine and other greens as well as partridge berries all along the way. As the projected plan for Shieling Forest develops there will be other features to attract visitors: a picnic area where families may come to enjoy the surroundings and a small amphitheater for lectures. The people of New Hampshire, especially those near Peterborough, are very fortunate, because this parcel of land called Shieling Forest will forever be there for everyone to enjoy.

After she gave over the land to the State, Elizabeth Yates still lived in her home until she moved to Heritage Heights in 1992. She would often go to the trails and loved to meet people there. She followed carefully all that the Forest Rangers were doing. Mr. Cullen brought up an interesting anecdote at the memorial service held in Concord after Mrs. McGreal's death. She called him in one day to reproach him that he had mowed part of the field. She said that hay was growing there and that was to continue as always. Mr. Cullen had brought his children that day. Squeals of laughter could be heard as she was talking to him. When she found out that the children were playing in the field, she realized that the field could be used as a place for children to play. She immediately changed her mind and said without delay: "Cut the whole field."

Even at Heritage Heights she was following what was going on. I had written to her prior to a visit I would have with her, that I thought the Mulberry Tree was no longer there. When I visited her, she immediately showed me a picture of the Mulberry Tree that had been taken by a friend quite recently and also said that another friend saw that the tree was producing berries. So much for my knowledge of Mulberry trees!

After she moved to Heritage Heights her home was also given to the State. No doubt the Forest Rangers will be using it as a dwelling for those who manage the program. It is my hope that some day this house could be kept as a memorial to Elizabeth Yates.

CHAPTER 8

AWARDS - CITATIONS - DEGREES

The following is a list of awards Elizabeth has won for some of her books. A statement of the purpose or the occasion of each one is appended:

THE NEW YORK HERALD TRIBUNE CHILDREN'S SPRING BOOK FESTIVAL AWARD, given to encourage the publication and sale of Children's books:

>   *Patterns on the Wall* in 1944.
>   *Amos Fortune, Free Man* in 1950.

THE JOHN NEWBERY MEDAL is awarded annually by the American Library Association for the most distinguished contribution to literature for children:

>   *Amos Fortune, Free Man* in 1951.

THE WILLIAM ALLEN WHITE CHILDREN'S BOOK AWARD is intended to encourage Kansas school children to read more and better books. From a master list of chosen books, each year the Kansas school children vote for the best book:

>   *Amos Fortune, Free Man* in 1953

>   ...

THE JUNIOR BOOKS AWARDS
The Boys Clubs of America established these awards to encourage wider reading among the members of boys' clubs across the nation:

A Place for Peter in 1953.

THE JANE ADDAMS CHILDREN'S BOOK AWARD
A Committee was created in 1953 by the United States Section of the Women's International League for Peace and Freedom, in honor of Jane Addams, one of the founders of the League. The purpose of this award is to encourage publication of books which are of literary merit and contain constructive themes, and as a means of recognizing and commending authors and publishers of such books:

Rainbow Round the World in 1955.

SARAH JOSEPHA HALE AWARD
To honor Sarah Josepha Hale, poet, novelist, editor, and crusader for women's rights, The Friends of the Richards Free Library in her birth-place, Newport, N.H. established this award in 1957. Each August a medal is given to someone distinguished in the field of literature and letters whose work reflects New England atmosphere or influence. A committee of distinguished men and women of the book world makes the decision

Elizabeth Yates, 1970.

PEABODY AWARD
The George Foster Peabody Awards, established in 1939 and first awarded in 1940, recognize distinguished achievement and meritorious service by radio and television networks, stations, producing organizations, cable

television organizations and individuals. They perpetuate the memory of the banker-philanthropist whose name they bear. The awards program is administered by Henry W. Grady College of Journalism and Mass Communication at the University of Georgia. Selections are made by the National Advisory Board upon recommendations of special screening sessions of the faculty.

*Skeezer, Dog with a Mission (*Film Version) 1983.

MEDAL OF THE AMERICAN HUMANE SOCIETY

This medal is given for its treatment of how pets are used in therapy for disturbed children.

Skeezer; Dog with *a Mission*

UNH PETTEE MEDAL AWARD

The Charles Holmes Pettee Medal was established in 1940 to recognize individuals who exhibit the rare devotion to service expressed by the life of the late Dean Pettee who served The University of New Hampshire unselfishly for 62 years as professor and dean until his death in 1938. The medal is awarded to a resident or former resident of the state in recognition of outstanding accomplishment or distinguished service in any form in the state, the nation or the world.

Elizabeth Yates, prolific New Hampshire Author, 1994

LAURA INGALLS WILDER AWARD

Association for Library Services to Children was established in 1954. Beginning in 1960, the award has been made every five years "to an author or illustrator whose books, published in the U.S., have over a period of years made a substantial and lasting contribution to literature for children." After 1980, will be given every three years.

In 1964 Elizabeth Yates

THE WOMEN STUDENTS OF HOWARD UNIVERSITY

Following a lecture given at Howard University, the Women Students presented a beautiful bronze plaque with the following engraved inscription: To Elizabeth Yates In appreciation of her distinguished biographies. The Women Students of Howard University 1958

NEW HAMPSHIRE WOMAN OF DISTINCTION CITATION FOR 1968.

presented by Alpha Delta Kappa International Honorary Sorority for Women Educators to ELIZABETH YATES

BEN THOMPSON CITATION UNIVERSITY OF NEW HAMPSHIRE

The University of New Hampshire gives this citation every five years to each of several prominent citizens "in recognition of a life and career marked by exceptionally meritorious service."

Elizabeth Yates McGreal received this citation April 20, 1959.

NATIONAL LIBRARY WEEK CERTIFICATE OF RECOGNITION

To Elizabeth Yates McGreal

1962 State Chairman for New Hampshire

The Steering Committee of National Library Week awards this certificate in recognition of the State Chairman's contribution to the success of the 1962 National Library Week Program.

VOLUNTEER ACHIEVEMENT AWARD. NEW HAMPSHIRE STATE LIBRARY

Division of Library Services to the Handicapped Presented this award to Elizabeth Yates McGreal April 19, 1976.

NEW HAMPSHIRE WOMAN OF DISTINCTION CITATION FOR 1968

Presented by Alpha Delta Kappa International Honorary Sorority for Women Educators to Elizabeth Yates. In recognition of her inspiring devotion to others, her high ideals, and her many outstanding achievements in the field of literature, which have brought honor and distinction to her, to her town and to New Hampshire.

NEW HAMPSHIRE LIBRARY TRUSTEES ASSOCIATION

Annual Citation to Elizabeth Yates McGreal for years of Outstanding Service. Given in 1977.

"The quiet strength and conscientious performance she has brought to her duties and to her work is the outward application of her deep, sensitive personal philosophy. Idealistic and giving of self, concerned for the quality of library service to all peoples by libraries of all sizes, her caring is constant and supportive."

THE NATIONAL COUNCIL ON THE AGING

Honors Elizabeth Yates for demonstrating through a lifetime of distinguished achievement the capacity of older Americans.

Given April 18, 1978.

THE PETERBOROUGH CHAMBER OF COMMERCE

Named Elizabeth Yates McGreal Citizen of the Year. 1980.

THE GOVERNOR'S AWARD OF DISTINCTION 1982.

During a ceremony at the Currier Gallery of Art, Elizabeth Yates McGreal was one of four recipients to receive this award. The following is the citation read at the ceremony:

"Elizabeth Yates McGreal of Peterborough, distinguished author of many books, generous citizen, public-spirited benefactor of worthy causes of all kinds. Her tireless work for the blind, her long years of able and devoted efforts on behalf of libraries...her gift to New Hampshire of Shieling Forest, forty-five acres of woodland, so splendid a gift as to be cited by the Governor, these are only a few of her achievements which inspired the Chamber of Commerce to name her citizen of the year in 1981."

AWARD HONORING THE STATE FOUNDERS

This Award Honoring the State Founders of Beta Alpha State, The Delta Kappa Gamma Society International, is given in Recognition of Personal and Professional contributions and Achievements which reflect the purposes of the Society. Given during the State Convention, Concord N.H. April 3, 1982 Marion R. Pounder, State President presented this award to Elizabeth Yates McGreal.

THE NEW HAMPSHIRE HOUSE OF REPRESENTATIVES

In 1987, Elizabeth Yates McGreal received an award for lifelong achievement from the New Hampshire House of Representatives.

RECOGNIZING NEW HAMPSHIRE'S AGELESS HEROES CERTIFICATE OF APPRECIATION

Awarded to ELIZABETH YATES McGREAL For demonstrating a commitment to healthy aging through Creativity/Vitality. Thank you for making NH a better place! signed:

> David A Jensen
>
> President and CEO - Blue Cross & Blue Shield of N.H.
>
> May 26, 1999.

HONORARY DEGREES

Elizabeth Yates received 8 Honorary Degrees from the colleges listed below:

> Aurora College, Aurora, Illinois, 1965.
>
> Eastern Baptist College, St Davids, Penn., 1966.
>
> Keene State College, Keene, NH, 1967.
>
> University of New Hampshire, Durham, NH, 1967.
>
> Ripon College, Ripon, Wisconsin, 1970.
>
> New England College, Henniker, NH, 1972.
>
> Rivier College, Nashua, NH, 1978.
>
> Franklin Pierce College, Rindge, NH, 1981.

CITATIONS FROM WRITERS' CONFERENCES

Elizabeth Yates participated in several Writers' Conferences. The following citation was given to her for her services at the Writers' Conferences at

Green Lake Wisconsin Christian Writers' and Editors' Conference, Green Lake Wisconsin, July 2-9, 1966:

> By action of the Board of the National Christian Writing Center and the Staff of the Conference, This award is given to ELIZABETH YATES In recognition of her outstanding literary skills which have been faithfully employed in the writing of notable books.

NOTES

Introduction

1. *New York Times,* December 17, 1950 p. 14.

2. *New York Herald Tribune Book Review,* October 1, 1950 p.5

Chapter 1.

1. Stanley Jasspon Kunitz and Howard Haycraft (eds *Junior Book of Authors* 2d ed. rev; New York: Wilson, 1951), 304.

2. Elizabeth Yates; "Ten Minutes a Day," *Chicago School Journal,* (January- February, 1952) 99.

3. Kunitz, p.303.

4. Elizabeth Yates, "Climbing Some Mountain in the Mind," *Horn Book Magazine.* (July- August, 1951) 268.

5. Elizabeth Yates, "How I began to Write," *Young Wings,* (May. 1943) 13

6. Elizabeth Yates, "Milestones in Reading," An unpublished talk from the Elizabeth Yates Collection at Boston University.

7. Elizabeth Yates, *My Diary, My World;* Philadelphia: Westminster Press, 1981: 15.

Chapter 2

1. Yates, *Chicago School Journal* (January-February, 1952): 99

2. Yates, "Milestones in Reading" an unpublished talk.

3. Yates, *Horn Book Magazine* (July-August, 1951): 268.

4. Yates, *Chicago School Journal,* (January-February, 1952) 99

5. Yates, *Horn Book Magazine* (July-August, 1951); 268.

6. Taken from the response to a questionnaire sent to Elizabeth Yates by the present writer.

Chapter 3

1. William McGreal, "Elizabeth Yates," *Horn Book Magazine,* (July-August, 1951): 262.
2. Taken from an unpublished talk given at the Public Library, Dover New Hampshire, May 1946. Elizabeth Yates Collection, Boston University.
3. Elizabeth Yates, *The Lighted Heart,* New York: Dutton, 1960: 54-55.
4. McGreal, *Horn Book Magazine (*July-August, 1951): 263-64.
5. Yates, *The Lighted Heart,* p 65.
6. Yates, *Up the Golden Stair,* New York: Dutton, 1966 (Forward)

Chapter 4

1. McGoldrick, Linda C. "Elizabeth Yates" *The New Hampshire Times,* 24 March, 1984: 18.
2. *New Hampshire State Library Biennial Report,* July 1, 1983- June 30, 1985: 5.
3. *Granite State Libraries,* August-September, 1989: 9.
4. Deborah Sumner, "Growing old is just growing up." *Keene Sentinel Magazine. (Observer)* August 25-31, 1990: 6-8.
5. McGoldrick, Linda C. "Elizabeth Yates," *New Hampshire Times,* 24 March, 1984: 17-19.
6. Ibid
7. "The McGreal Sight Center," *The New Hampshire Association for the Blind,* Special Dedication Edition, 15 June, 1985.

8. Ibid.

9. *New Hampshire Association for the Blind.,* "McGreal Sight Center Ribbon Cutting: Reminiscences of Elizabeth Y. McGreal. Annual Report 1998.

10. Dennis Paiste, "Helpers of Blind Dedicate Building to Bill McGreal," *Concord Monitor,* 15 June, 1985.

11. "The William and Elizabeth Yates McGreal Society for the endowment of the New Hampshire Association for the Blind." Newsletter, Sept. 1992.

12. Maria Cimino, "Elizabeth Yates," *Wilson Library Bulletin* (February, 1948): 422.

CHAPTER 5

1. McGoldrick, Linda Clark; *Nora S. Unwin, Artist and Wood Engraver,"* Dublin, NH. William L. Bauhan, 1990: 62

2. Ibid. pp. 38-39.

3. Ibid. pp. 39-40.

4. Elizabeth Yates, "Portrait of an Artist", *Horn Book Magazine* (March, 1950): 139.

5. McGoldrick, *Nora S. Unwin*...p. 116.

6. Ibid. p. 116.

7. Ibid, p. 116.

8. Ibid, p. 116.

Chapter 6

1. Taken from an unpublished talk at the Public Library, Dover NH, May,1946.

2. Yates, *Horn Book Magazine* 27, 273.

3. *New York Times,* February 15, 1959: 2.

4. James C. MacCampbell, "The Work of Elizabeth Yates," *Elementary English (*November, 1952): 381.

5. Cimino, *Wilson Library Journal* XXII p.422.

6. Taken from notes in the Elizabeth Yates Collection, Boston University.

7. Ibid.

8. Isaiah 40: 9.

9. II Chronicles 31:21

10. Myra K. Campbell, "Elizabeth Yates," *North Country Libraries,* (January-February, 1956): 12

11. Dan Thomasson, "'Greener Fields' delights audience," clipping from the Elizabeth Yates Collection at Boston University. n.d.

BIBLIOGRAPHY OF WORKS
BY ELIZABETH YATES
ARRANGED CHRONOLOGICALLY

ANNOTATED LIST OF BOOKS

Most of the following annotations have been quoted from the *Book Review Digest:* these are indicated by the abbreviations B.R.D. The source of other annotations quoted is also given. Where no source is indicated, the annotations are the author's. Only foreign editions that could be traced have been listed. There is no claim that this is a complete list of all editions.

1. *High holiday.* London: A.C. Black, 1938.

...the story of an English boy and girl, Michael and Merry Lamb, fourteen and thirteen years old, who go with a young uncle to Switzerland and have their first experiences in mountain climbing through a whole summer there...A real feeling for all the aspects of mountain climbing is given and the effort and care and pains which must be put into it.

Horn Book Magazine, Jan. 1939. 31

2. *Climbing Higher, and Iceland Adventure.* London: A.C. Black, 1938. *Quest in the Northland.* New York: Knopf, 1940. (American edition of *Climbing Higher*) Toronto: Ryerson Press, 1940 *Island Adventure (*Journey Books). Greenville: SC: Bob Jones University Press, 1997.

Two English children accompany their uncle on a trip to Iceland. They travel widely thru the island, and learn about the people, their manners and customs. Told in fiction form for ages ten to fourteen.

B.R.D. 1940, p. 1019, 52

3. *Hans and Frieda in the Swiss Mountains:* Wide World Story Book Series. New York: Thomas Nelson, 1939.

Frieda, a city girl on a visit to the mountains, proves to her cousin Hans, that she can keep up with any boy. The end of the summer brings wonderful surprises for the two cousins.

4. *Haven for the Brave.* New York: Knopf, 1941. Toronto: Ryerson Press, 1941.

Story of an English brother and sister in their teens, who come to America for the duration of the war. They go first to a farm in Canada, and then to New Hampshire, where they are to stay. Their adventures include mountain climbing and a forest fire.

5. *Around the Year in Iceland* (Illustrated by Jon Nielson). Boston: Heath, 1942. (New World Neighbors) One of a series of sixteen Geography books, written by persons who have traveled or lived in the countries described. Also illustrated by a person who knows the country well.

6. *Under the Little Fir, and other Stories.* (Illustrated by Nora S. Unwin). New York: Coward-McCann, 1942. London: Hutchinson Juvenile Books, 1944.

Six imaginative stories first written for the children in a London school and told in the story-telling hour. The title story is a retelling of the legend of peace among all animals on Christmas Eve.

B.R.D. 1942, p. 857.

7. *Patterns on the Wall*, New York: Knopf, 1943. London: Cassell, 1941. Published as *The Journeyman*, Bob Jones University Press, 1990.

New England in the early years of the nineteenth century is the scene of this novel for young readers. It is the story of Jared Austin, at first, apprentice to a journeyman painter, and then painter on his own. The climax comes in the cold summer of 1816

B.R.D. 1943, p. 857

Other Editions: Toronto: Ryerson Press, 1943

New York: Aladdin, 1943.

Toronto: Saunders, 1953.

8. *Mountain Born* Illustrated by Nora S. Unwin, New York: Coward-McCann 1943, London: Hutchinson Juvenile Books, 1954. Bob Jones University Press, Pennant Series, 1993.

Story of a little shepherd lad, and the lamb which he raised from a cosset, to become the leader of the flock.

B.R.D. 1943. p. 896.

9. *Wind of Spring.* New York: Coward McCann, 1945. Toronto: Longsman, 1945: London: Cassell, 1948.

The Story of Susie Minton, who in the last decade of the nineteenth century started out on her life work as a maid "in service." Her life in the great houses of England, and those not so great, is depicted through three wars, The Boer War in which she lost her lover, the first World War in which she lost her son; and the Second World War. Susie's character, which was staunch and fine to begin with, developed steadily until even the stern, unbending woman for whom she had worked so long, finally realized how great a treasure Susie Minton had been.

B.R.D. 1945 p. 797.

10. *Nearby*: a novel. New York: Coward-McCann, 1947. Toronto: Longsman 1947. London: Cassell & Co., 1950. Reprinted by Bob Jones University Press, 1991.

A young girl chooses to teach in a rural school, in a New England community called *Nearby.* There she finds not only opportunity to put into effect her social ideals but, eventually, personal happiness as well.

B.R.D. 1947 p. 995.

11. *Once in a Year: a Christmas Story.* Illustrated by Nora S. Unwin. New York: Coward-McCann, 1947. Toronto: Longsman, 1947. Reprinted by Upper Room Books, 1991.

Using as a framework Christmas Eve in a snow-covered farm where the mother lights a Christmas candle and reads to her little boy, the story of the first Christmas retells with warmth and sympathy two of the loveliest Christmas legends, of the blossoming forest and of the animals at midnight

B.R.D. 1947 p. 995

12. *Beloved Bondage* New York: Coward-McCann, 1948. Toronto: Longsman, 1948.

John Bennet, a furniture salesman, married beautiful Althea Trainer, the daughter of a wealthy family, and almost at once discovered that Althea was subject to some psychopathic block which made her unwilling to consummate the marriage. For many years he cared for her patiently, until thru her desire to help a crippled friend, Althea was cured. John's own salvation was in the hands of an understanding elderly librarian.

B.R.D. 1948, p.948.

13. *The Young Traveler in the USA* London: Phoenix House, 1948.

The travels of a young Englishman to the United States of the 40's. His visit to a relative takes him through most of the country. The book is illustrated by many photographs.

Other editions.:

London: British Book Center, 1951.

London: Dent. 1951. Paderbom: Schoningh, 1951.

German edition: Mainz: Verlag Styria, 1951.

Japanese edition: Shonen Shojo Sekai no Tabi. Tokyo: Kikku Sha, 1958

Dutch edition: De Jonge Reizigers in de Verenigde Staten Van Amerika. Amsterdam: Van der Peet, 1960, 1963

Hebrew edition: Masseot Ha-Tayyar Ha-Zair Be-Arzot Ha-Berit.

14. *Amos Fortune, Free Man.* Illustrated by Nora S. Unwin. New York: Aladdin, 1951.

Amos Fortune was the son of an African chief, brought to this country as a slave in 1725, when he was a boy of fifteen. This is his story, as gathered from old accounts. At the age of fifty he managed to buy his own freedom. He died in 1801, a man of property, and is buried in Jaffrey, New Hampshire. For older boys and girls.

B.R.D. 1950, p. 1001

Other editions:

Toronto: Saunders, 1950.

New York: Dutton, 1956.

New York: Dell (Yearling Book) Paper ed. 1971.

Penguin (Puffin Books) 1989.

Amos Fortune has an amazing vitality. A record has been made (from a dramatization) by Miller Brody Productions (New York), and a film by Station WABC-WETV in Atlanta, GA. The Smithsonian is including him in a special room, and his sales have averaged well over 10,000 a year since 1950.

15. *Guardian Heart.* New York: Coward-McCann, 1950. Toronto: Longsman, 1950. London: Museum Press, 1952.

The love story of a sturdy unspoiled girl of the New Hampshire hills, the descendant of a long line of pioneers, and the young college trained mill owner. His aristocratic mother tries to make Freely over in her own image, but the girl remains true to herself and the future is promising for all of them.

B.R.D. 1950, p. 1001.

German Edition: Der *Heimliche Graud.* Frauenfeld: Verlag Huber, 1952.

16. *Children of the Bible.* Illustrated by Nora S. Unwin. New York: Aladdin,1950. Reprinted paper ed. Cobblestone Pub. 1996. (Illustrated by Chris Wold Dyreed) 1999.

> Fifteen brief stories about children in the Bible. Based on the King James version, including some direct quotations. David, Samuel, Moses, Jairus's daughter, the little serving maid of Naaman, and two stories about Jesus, are among these tales.
>
> for ages 6-10.   B.R.D. 1951, P. 977.

Other editions: Toronto: Saunders, 1951.

> London: Meiklejohn. 1951.
>
> New York: Dutton, 1958.
>
> Cape Town: Hollandsch Afrikaansche
>
> Uitgevers Maatschappij, 1970.

17. *Brave Interval.* New York: Coward-McCann, 1952. Toronto: Longsman, 1952. London: Andrew Dakers, 1953.

> Five people, each facing a problem, take a pack trip in the wilderness of the Smoky Mountains, accompanied by a wise leader and two guides. The trip brings its quota of hardships, but also five contented people back to the starting point.

B.R.D. 1952 p. 986.

18. *A Place for Peter.* Illustrated by Nora S. Unwin. New York: Coward-McCann, 1952. Toronto: Longsman, 1952. Reprinted Paper ed. (Pennant Series) Bob Jones University Press, 1994. Light Line Series, 1991.

A sequel to *Mountain Born (*Book Review Digest 1943).

It is the story of a New Hampshire farm boy who proves he can take responsibility when his mother is called away from home for a long period. Grades 5 to 8.

B.R.D. 1952, p. 986.

19. *David Livingstone.* Row Peterson, 1953.

The son of a poor clerk. He went to work at the age of 10. After schooling himself he attended medical classes and chose to spread the Gospel while healing the sick in distant lands.

20. *Hue and Cry.* New York: Coward-McCann, 1953. Toronto: Longsman, 1953. Greensville, S.C.: Bob Jones University Press, 1990. (Light Line Series) 1991.

The setting of the novel is New Hampshire in 1836-37, a largely rural society in which the voluntary organization, the Hue and Cry, kept a close watch for horse thieves. The Austin family consisted of three teenagers, two boys and the deaf girl, Melody, in addition to the parents, Jared and Janet. It was part of the Hue and Cry network, and in due time it collected the reward for the return of *Blue Lightning*.
Chicago Sunday Tribune, Sept. 27, 1953.

German edition; *Reiter des Rechts.* Frauenfeld: Huber, 1954.

21. *Rainbow Round the World: a Story of UNICEF.* endpaper drawing by Dirk Gringhuis; il. by Betty Alden. Indianapolis: Bobbs, 1954.

An American boy, aged eleven, accompanies a representative of the United Nations on a three-weeks trip around the world. Gradually he learns of the benefits of UNICEF to the children in need in the countries he visits, from Arabia and India to Japan and the Philippines. For Grades 5 to 9.

B.R.D. 1955, p.1003.

Other English editions: Toronto: McClelland, 1954.

Bangalore, India: The P.T.I. Book Depot, n.d.

German edition *John Fliegt Um Die Welt.* Frauenfeld: Huber, 1956.

Bengali edition, Calcutta: Mitra & Fohsch, 1954.

Sinhalese edition, *Lama Lokaya.* Colombo, Ceylon: Gunaratna & Co. 1961.

22. *Prudence Crandall: Woman of Courage.* New York: Aladdin, 1955. Honesdale PA; Boyds Mills Press, 1996. Reprinted for Society for Developmental Education, 1990. Peterborough, NH.

The life story of a young Quakeress who in 1833 opened her school to 'young ladies and little misses of color' and was persecuted for her stand by the towns people. But Prudence Crandall, faithful to her convictions and even though she had to give up her Connecticut school, opened other schools with her husband's help. For young readers.

B.R.D. 1955, p. 1003

Other editions: New York: Dutton, 1958, 1965.

Toronto: Smithers, 1955.

23. *The Carey Girl.* decorations by Georg Hartmann. New York: Coward-McCann, 1956. Toronto: Longsman, 1956.

After an unhappy childhood, when she had lived with first one then the other of her divorced parents, Kit Carey, at twenty-two thought she had found love. When that too failed she took poison. The doctor who treated her, and his understanding wife, were the ones who gave her courage for the few days of life she had left.

B.R.D. 1956, p. 1033

German edition *Kit Und Die Wildganse.* Frauenfeld: Huber, 1957.

24. *Gifts of True Love.* Illustrated by Nora S. Unwin. Wallingford, PA.: Pendle Hill, 1958, 1983.

Based on the Christmas Carol the author goes through the twelve months of the year accentuating a special gift for each month.

25. *Pebble in a Pool; The Widening Circles of Dorothy Canfield Fisher's Life.* New York: Dutton, 1958. Toronto: Smithers,1958. Published as: *The Lady from Vermont: Dorothy Canfield Fisher's Life and World,* Greene, 1971.

Appearing almost simultaneously with the death of Mrs. Fisher, this biography presents a fitting summary of a long and rewarding life. Miss Yates has not attempted to give us a scholarly interpretation of Mrs. Fisher's works and their place in American Literature. Rather, this is a warm and admiring portrait of a woman best known as a writer and educator, but here portrayed also in her role as wife and mother.

North Country Libraries. February, 1959, 5.

26. *The Lighted Heart.* Pen drawings by Nora S. Unwin. New York: Dutton, 1960. Toronto: Clarke, Irwin, 1960. reprinted, Dublin, N.H. William Bauhan, 1974.

Miss Yates, with vivid word-pictures of their home and surrounding countryside in Peterborough, N.H., shares in this personal narrative the many problems that arise when her husband, Bill McGreal, loses his sight. Their solutions of these problems are shared experiences met with courage, love, and faith. Miss Yates' fans, as well as many others, will find inspiration and understanding invaluable for facing their own crises. Lovingly illustrated by their good friend and neighbor, Nora Unwin.

North Country Libraries, Sept. - Oct., 1960.

27. The *Next Fine Day:* with line drawings by Nora S. Unwin. New York: Day, 1962. Toronto: Longsman, 1962. London: Dent, 1964. 2nd ed. Jordan Susette, ed., Greenville, SC.: Bob Jones University Press, 1994.

Kent Conner is the only child of widowed, hard-working Maidey Connor. He is a lonely English boy of 11 or so, who calls himself 'Mr. Nobody' and who searches for beauty and comfort in the world around him. Then on one fine day, his search brings him not only the beauty of the heron in flight but also the friendship of the artist, John Rivven. Kent is on his way toward filling the gap in his lonely heart and toward the discovery that as surely as the herons return to Chilham on or before St. Valentine's Day, just so surely does each year bring more that is good than not.

Library Journal, Dec. 1, 1961, 18.

Spanish edition: Buenos Aires: Comision Rioplatense de Literatura Christians, n.d.

28. *Someday, You'll Write.* New York: Dutton, 1962. Paper ed. 1969.
Bob Jones University, Pennant Series. Debbie Parker, ed. 1995. reprinted, Society for Developmental Education, 1990. Peterborough, NH.

Written for young people who are contemplating a writer's career. Packed with ideas and suggestions that can help a youngster prepare for the future.

29. *Howard Thurman: Portrait of a Practical Dreamer.* New York: Day, 1964.

'Our dreams are our thing...They become for us the bearers of the new possibility, the enlarged horizon, the greater hope.' For Howard Thurman, minister, teacher, author, the dream had always been the realization in life of the unity of all life, the oneness of mankind; and the hope—the hope for a community undivided by creed and dogma in which this might be made manifest. In tracing Howard Thurman's life from the Negro ghetto boyhood of Daytona Beach Florida to the deanship of the Marsh Chapel at Boston University, Elizabeth Yates relates the growth and articulation of that dream. It is a warm and gentle telling which succeeds in bringing to the reader a sense of the gentle but grand strength of a man who bears witness to his convictions. *North Country Libraries* Jan. - Feb., 1965, 22.

30. *Sam's Secret Journal* Illustrated by Allan Eitzen, New York: Friendship Press, 1964.

Written in diary form and based on the life of a boy who did not live to reach manhood, this is the intimate and inspiring story of a soul who tried to please God.

31. *Carolina's Courage* Illustrated by Nora S. Unwin. New York: Dutton, 1964. Toronto: Clarke, Irwin, 1964. Greenville SC.: Bob Jones University, Light Line Series, 1989.

An account of a pioneer family, the Putnams, and their journey from New Hampshire to the Nebraska territory in search of more fertile farmland. We follow them behind their team of oxen, hoping they will cover their hundred miles a week...it is through the eyes of Carolina, the small daughter, that we follow most of the travel; and it is also through a sacrifice of hers that the family safely passes its crisis. As they approach the Platte River the book ends; we know they will reach their goal...Ages 9 - 12.

N.Y. Times Book Review, Nov. 29, 1964, p.34.

Other editions: *Carolina and the Indian Doll.* London: Methuen, 1965.
Afrikaans edition: *Carolina en die Rooihuidpop.* Cape Town: Hollandsch Uitgevers Maatschappij, 1968.

32. *Up the Golden Stair; An Approach to a Deeper Understanding of Life Through Personal Sorrow.* New York: Dutton, 1966. Toronto: Clarke, Irwin, 1966; reprinted, Dublin, NH: William Bauhan, 1977. reprinted, Nashville TN: Upper Room Books, 1990...

Miss Yates writes simply and honestly about the reality of death and the necessity of facing it calmly and creatively. There is real moral fiber and sensitivity in this discussion, which obviously owes much to the author's personal experience with sorrow. The book is further enhanced by an appendix containing poems on the subject by various authors.

North Country Libraries. May-June, 1966, 64.

33. *Is there a Doctor in the Barn? A day in the Life of Forrest F. Tenney, D.V.M..* Illustrated by Guy Fleming. New York: Dutton, 1966. reprinted,

Dublin: William Bauhan, 1977. Paper ed. Madison, WI: North Country Press, 1994.

With skill and compassion, humor and kindness, Dr. Tenney of Peterborough treats ailing animals in barns and clinic in this warm account of one typical day in this life as a New Hampshire veterinarian. Elizabeth Yates writes of her neighbor of 20 years with admiration for both his human qualities and his ability as a doctor. Technical details of his treatment of farm animals and pets provide fascinating reading for the uninitiated as well as for young people interested in veterinary medicine as a career. Interwoven with the story is a description of Dr. Tenney's boyhood and youth in Antrim, NH, which evokes a mellow and tender picture of rural life in the early part of the century. To gather material for her book, the author accompanied the doctor on his rounds and even assisted in giving anesthesia when needed. A delightful biography, written with understanding of the man and his profession and of the people and animals whose lives he affects. Highly recommended for all adult and young adult collections.

North Country Libraries, May-June, 1966, 94.

34. *An Easter Story.* Illustrated by Nora S. Unwin. New York: Dutton, 1967. Toronto: Clarke, Irwin, 1967.

Young Debra had to spend a four-day Easter holiday alone with Cousin Con in the country, because on Palm Sunday her beloved foster brother, Dan, was seriously injured in an accident, and her parents had to stay in the city. Horror at the accident, grief, shock and fear for the outcome absorbed Debra. Cousin Con, an unusual woman who had known sorrow but had come to terms with life, wisely interested Debra in preparations for Easter. Daily calls from the city finally gave the good news that Dan was expected to live. Woven through the story are innumerable bits of information about the great Easter feast, pagan lore, Jewish custom, and early Christian traditions that blend Easter customs familiar to all today. A Christian, but not sectarian spirit, and sentiment, but not sentimentality, distinguish the story. The illustrations by Nora Unwin are perfectly suited to the text.

North Country Libraries, May-June, 1967, 104.

35. *With Pipe, Paddle, and Song: A Story of the French-Canadian Voyageurs circa 1750.* Illustrated with a map and line drawing by Nora S. Unwin. New York: Dutton, 1968. Toronto: Clarke, Irwin, 1968. reprint ed. Bathgate ND: Bethlehem ND 1999.

Engrossing historical novel presents a warm, vivid account of a by-gone era. Guillaume Puissante, a French-Indian half-breed, makes his first journey into the north woods as a voyageur. His ability to sing the old French ballads makes him popular with companions as they paddle canoes through lakes and streams to trade with Indians. Disaster overtakes Guillaume in treacherous rapids, and an exciting romantic interlude brings maturity and an understanding of life and love to the young voyageur before he returns to his companions. Thirteen voyageur songs set to music, with lyrics in both French and English, are included at the end of the book.

North Country Libraries, July-Aug., 1968, 144.

French edition: Quebec: Editions Jeunesse, 1970.
German edition: Stuttgart: Schwabenverlag A G, 1970.

36. *On That Night:* 14 halftones by James Barkley. New York: Dutton, 1969.

The legend that says on Christmas Eve lost things are found again is epitomized in six short stories of troubled human beings who attend the traditional Candlelight Service in their church, visit the Manger, light their candles, and find hope and courage where there was none before. A spiritual and moving story of how the love and beauty characterizing the Christmas season can open the human heart, told in a direct, yet intimate and compassionate manner. Black and white illustrations have a mystical quality subtly and beautifully depicting the characters, first in despair, then in hope. For all collections of Christmas books.

North Country Libraries, Nov.-Dec., 1969, 25.

Abridged edition: *Reader's Digest,* Dec, 1969, 227-266.
The Australian Women's Weekly, Sydney, Australia, Dec. 24, 1965, 499-65.
Hjemmet. Oslo, Norway. A Norwegian edition appeared in this magazine, Dec., 1970.

37. *New Hampshire.* New York: Coward-McCann, 1970.

Though it is small in size, New Hampshire's scenic mountains, thick pine forests and countryside of farmland, lakes and rivers make it one of our nation's most beautiful states. The first of the thirteen colonies to declare its independence, New Hampshire has continued in the spirit of freedom and individualism. New Hampshire natives are proud of this spirit and many of their own words add depth and flavor to this book...Elizabeth Yates, author of many children's books and longtime resident of the state, presents a vivid and compelling picture of New Hampshire.

Publisher's Note

38. *Sarah Whitcher's Story:* Illustrated by Nora S. Unwin. New York: Dutton, 1971. Greenville SC: Bob Jones University Press, Pennant Series, 1994.

Sarah Whitcher was lost in the New Hampshire woods during early pioneer days. Men from miles around came in to join in the search for her, but after a day or two, they began to feel that the search was almost hopeless. A miracle was needed to find her in that big wilderness forest. Publisher's Note

39. *Skeezer: Dog with a Mission:* Illustrated by Joan Dresscher. Irving-on-Hudson, NY: Harvey House, 1973. reprinted, New York: Avon, 1974.

The true story of a dog trained to help emotionally disturbed children at the University of Michigan Medical Center. Told in a Matter-of-fact manner that should give this book a large audience. Grades 5 up.

Teacher, Feb., 1975, 115.

[Was adapted as a Television film by National Broadcasting Company (NBC) 1981.]

40. *The Road through Sandwich Notch:* Brattleboro, VT: Stephen Greene, 1973. Reprinted: Society for the Protection of New Hampshire Forests, 1987.

Sandwich Notch, a pass in the New Hampshire White Mountains, was once a busy road for farmers' commerce; but the early settlers have gone and the forest has again claimed the land. Now, however, without some form of public protection, the road stands to be commercially developed for vacation homes and recreational access. Sandwich Notch is not a large area, nor one of major historical value. So, to discover for herself why this road should be preserved, Yates and her dog Sir Gibbie walked the nine-mile length and back. This remarkable and understated account tells of their journey to woodlands and old burial places which recreate a sense of continuity with the serene past. The message in this conservation appeal lies in the road itself—an example in miniature of what is happening all over the country—and Yates is its able translator. A desirable addition to conservation collections.—Anita Mygaard, Mountaineer Foundation Library, Seattle, Washington.

Library Journal Dec. 1, 1973, 3574.

41. *We the People:* Illustrated by Nora Unwin; published [for] the Regional Center for Educational Training, Hanover, NH. Taftsville, VT: Countryman Press, 1975.

A young wife holds her family together while the husband goes off to fight in the American Revolution. There are 39 gracefully written pages of the same genre as *April Morning* but seen through the eyes of a woman. Grade 4 and up.

Teacher, March, 1975, 113.

42. *A Book of Hours:* art by Carol Aymar Armstrong, (Crossroad Book) Norton, Conn.: Vineyard Books Inc., 1976. reprinted: Nashville TN: Upper Room Books, 1989.

Like and unlike Medieval Books of Hours, Elizabeth Yates' *A Book of Hours* embraces the ordinariness of everyday life and finds it holy. For those who feel close to God and for those who would like to, *A Book of*

Hours represents the unselfish sharing of a serene and mature faith. [Large Type ed. pap.: New York: Walker Pub. 1985.

43. *Call it Zest: the Vital Ingredient after Seventy:* Brattleboro, VT: Greene, 1977.

Here's a book to ameliorate the anxiety and apprehension experienced by thousands as "ripe old age" approaches. It contains dynamic profiles of individuals who, though statistically retired, have found that being over seventy need not retire one from active useful productive living.

Publisher's Note

Large Print edition:

Boston: G.K. Hall, 1979.

44. *The Seventh One:* Illustrated by Diana Charles. New York: Walker, 1978.

"Jeanne Gardner told me she had long felt the need for a book that would help young people to think of aging and death as parts of the natural process of life. The idea took hold of me and I went back over the years of dogs I had known—The sealyham who went with me to New York and into the first years of that new life in London, the Scotties who had been such a part of Shieling, then the Skelties, coming up to the present with my magnificent German Shepherd. It was there that the story began as a Seeing Eye Dog and a young blind boy took it over. It was not my story but Tom Wilson's, a character I invented. At the start he is a young boy with his first dog and he lives through more than sixty years of different dogs. The end is the beginning as a German Shepherd and a blind boy come into his life. I felt enriched, almost ennobled, by the memories brought back of all the dogs I had known through all the years."

Elizabeth Yates, *Something About the Author.*
Autobiography Series, Volume 6, p. 292.

45. *Silver Lining: a Novella.* Illustrated by A.L. Morrio Canaan, NH: Phoenix, 1981.

Seeking shelter on a night of wild weather, an oddly assorted group of people come to know each other. Was it fear of the storm or of the future which gave such intensity to their meeting that in discovering each other they discovered themselves and their needs? Bart's rustic home on the slope of a mountain is the setting, the great oak that towers nearby is the uncertainty. The characters reveal their true selves, safe in the assurance that they will never see each other again while some wonder if they will ever see the morning.

Publisher's Note

46. *My Diary - My World.* Philadelphia: Westminster Press, 1981.

Most of the entries in a book in diary form are based on the real diary kept by Elizabeth Yates from 1917, when she was twelve, until 1925 when she left home to settle in New York to become a published writer; the entries here are selected, and they are supplemented by material from notebooks

B.R.D. 1981, p. 1572.

47. *My Widening World* [autobiographical}. Philadelphia: Westminster Press, 1983.

This is the second book on the autobiography of Elizabeth Yates. It is her journal as she begins her career as a writer in New York City. The account is climaxed by her marriage to Bill McGreal and the beginning of a new life in England.

48. *One writer's Way.* Philadelphia: Westminster Press, 1984.

This completes the trilogy of the autobiography of Elizabeth Yates based on her diaries for the years 1931 through 1951. Here we follow the author as she succeeds to publish her first children's book and we live with her through the poignant personal tragedy of her husband's blindness. The conclusion of this account brings the couple to a new home on a century-old farm in Peterborough NH.

49. *Sound Friendships; The Story of Willa and her Hearing Ear Dog.* Woodstock, VT: The Countryman Press, 1987. 2nd ed. 1988. reprint edition: Leaman Christina, ed. Greenville SC: Bob Jones University Press, Pennant Series, 1992.

The Hearing Ear Dog Program was begun in 1975 to assist the deaf and severely hearing impaired. In a fashion similar to the way Seeing Eye Dogs aid the blind, the dogs are trained to recognize ordinary household sounds (smoke alarms, tea-kettles, doorbells, etc.) and more specific needs (owner's name, a crying baby, sirens in traffic, etc.) Yates illustrates the success of this exciting program with a heartwarming tale involving Willa, 24-year-old woman who lost her hearing at age 14, and her dog, Honey. Thorough coverage of how the dogs are trained and rewarded and how the deaf person must adjust to this program, is neatly blended with a sensitive portrayal of Willa's growing self-reliance and accomplishments.

Booklist, April 1, 1987, p. 1163.

50. *Spanning Time. A Diary Keeper Becomes a Writer.* Carolyn P. Yoder, ed. Peterborough NH: C Cobblestone Pub. 1996.

A compilation of the three diary books of Elizabeth Yates: *My Diary, My World, (1981)* along with the two sequels: *My Widening World* (1983) and *One Writer's Way* (1984.) This autobiography covers the years 1917-1951.The predominant theme in this work is the persistent desire and effort to become a writer. This edition has been enhanced with many photographs taken from the author's photo album.

51. *Open the Door; a Gathering of Poems and Prose Pieces.* Hopkinton NH: New Hampshire Antiquarian Society, 1999.

"Elizabeth Yates' writing is rich with her observations of the natural world. It is a world from which she takes inspiration and which she has done much to protect." Jane A. Dally.

"Elizabeth sees with her heart. Then she brings us to see what she sees, to know what she's been given to know, 'announced' in these collected poems. Mary Lynn Ray

ANNOTATED LIST OF BOOKS
COMPILED OR EDITED

by Elizabeth Yates

1. *Gathered Grace; A Short Selection of G. Macdonald's Poems;* With a Biographical Sketch, compiled by Elizabeth Yates; with a forward by Lucia C. Coulson; wood engravings by Nora S. Unwin. Cambridge: W. Heffer & Sons, 1938. 129p.

2. Tregarthen Enys. *Piskey Folk: A Book of Cornish Legends;* collected by Elizabeth Yates; illustrated with photographs by William McGreal. New York: Day, 1940. 203p. Toronto: McClelland.

    Collection of legends of Cornwall in which the little folk—the Piskies— appear and play important parts. The stories were discovered in 1939, by the editor and her husband, among the papers of the Cornish folklorist Enys Tregarthen. Illustrated with photographs of Cornwall. Glossary.

B.R.D. 1940, pp. 924-25.

3. Tregarthen, Enys. *The Doll Who Came Alive;* edited by Elizabeth Yates and illustrated by Nora S. Unwin. New York: Day, 1940. Toronto: Ryerson Press, 1941. London: Faber & Faber, n.d.

    Imaginative story of Cornwall for girls from eight to ten. Little Jyd was unhappy and neglected until a sailor man gave her a little Dutch doll. With a doll to love Jyd was completely happy. Later when the doll came to life the two escaped from Jyd's dreary home and went to live in fairy land.

B.R.D. 1942, p. 781.

Other editions: Toronto: Ryerson Press, 1942

London: Faber & Faber, n.d.

New York: Day, 1972.

4. *Joseph; the King James Version of a Well-Loved Tale;* arranged by Elizabeth Yates, il. by Nora S. Unwin. New York: Knopf, 1947.

Pleasure in the beauty of the Bible narrative is here enhanced by the designed pages and the distinguished engravings by Nora Unwin. The greatness of the tale itself will be more likely to speak to young people in this form than in its conventional position in the book of Genesis, interspersed with unrelated matter.

Horn Book Magazine, (may, 1947), 217.

5. Tregarthen, Enys. *The White Ring;* edited by Elizabeth Yates; with illustrations by Nora S. Unwin. New York: Harcourt, 1949.

An old Cornish legend, told for grades three to five. It is about the tiny girl Nan found on the shore by a kindly old man, whose whole life was devoted to caring for small injured animals. For years Nan helped him until finally both she and her beloved 'Grandfer' assumed their rightful forms and went back to Fairyland as its king and queen.

B.R.D. 1949, p. 72.

6. Bible. Whole. Selections. *The Christmas Story;* arranged by Elizabeth Yates; il. with wood engravings by Nora S. Unwin. New York: Aladdin, 1949

The Christmas story is here told in relevant verses chosen from the Bible, beginning with the Prophets, and ending with the book of John and Revelation.

B.R.D. 1949, p. 72

7. *Your Prayers and Mine;* arranged by Elizabeth Yates; decorations by Nora S. Unwin. Boston: Houghton, 1954. Toronto: T. Allen, 1954.

A collection of prayers taken from the Old and New Testaments, from Saint Augustine and Saint Francis, from the Rabbi Gamaliel, Socrates, and Mohammed, from ancient Gaelic runes, the Navajo Indian, and the Breton fisherman.

Publisher's Note.

8. Macdonald, George. *Sir Gibbie;* edited and with a forword by Elizabeth Yates. Abridged edition. New York: Dutton, 1963.

A revised edition of the Scottish writer's novel, originally published in 1878. The editor states that she has "cut the original *Sir Gibbie* almost by half, taking out the pages that were a digression from the story, and...'translated' the Scotch dialect into English, except for certain flavorful words which have long been familiar." (Forward) The story opens with young Sir Gibbie running about the Scottish city, caring for his beloved father and leading a cheerful existence. On the death of his father Gibbie flees from the city [In the countryside] he is taken into the home of Robert and Janet Grant and there he begins to learn to read [the Bible] and write. The example of Janet and her concern for a literal interpretation of the life of Christ is one of the most profound of influences on Gibbie through his future. Returned to the city as an heir,

Gibbie finished his college education and puts his fortune to use in helping others.

Best Sellers, (September 15, 1963), 210

Other editions: Toronto: Clarke, Irwin, 1963.

London: Black & Son, 1967.

New York: Schocken Books, 1979.

9. Macdonald, George. *The Last Princess* or *The Wise Woman* with four color plates and line drawings in the text by D.J. Watkins-Pitchford. New York: Dutton, 1965.

This story, "also known as *A Double Story and the Wise Woman,* has itself been lost. Soon after [the author's] death in 1905, it mysteriously disappeared from his publishers' lists on both sides of the Atlantic and has remained unavailable until now...[It] concerns two fearsome children, Princess Rosamond and Agnes, a shepherd girl. Both are badly corrupted by the illusion that they are SOMEBODY...Both girls are 'treated in a manner of speaking, by the Wise Woman...[who] employs drastic means with Rosamond...Rosamond grows compassionate and for the first time tastes the sweetness of humility...There is, however, no help for Agnes...In the closing scene, the Wise Woman wrathfully blames the two sets of parents for the ruin of Rosamond and Agnes. She punishes the king and queen by striking them blind, while the shepherd and his wife are condemned to live with Agnes, who looks white as death and mean as sin...

B.R.D. 1966 p. 754.

79

SHORT STORIES

"C'est la guerre," *The Smokers' Companion,* I (September, 1927)

"Robert's Treasure Hunt," *Christian Science Monitor,* February 29, 1932.

"The Cuckoo Clock," *Christian Science Monitor,* August 13, 1934, p. 6.

"Under the Little Fir, *Christian Science Monitor,* December 17, 1934.

"A Tale Told in the Sand," *Christian Science Monitor,* May 17, 1937, p. 8.

"The Little Hen's Thank You," *Christian Science Monitor,* June 1, 1937: 10

"Golden Heritage," *Story Parade,* (Aug. 1938), 35-45. Also in Nolen, Barbara (comp.) *Children of America.* Chicago: John Winston, 1939. pp.139-150. Also in Wagenhein, Harold H. *Our Reading Heritage; Wide Horizons.* New York: Henry Holt, 1958. pp. 62-69. Also in Thomas Aquinas, Sister M. *This is our Heritage.* Toronto: Ginn, n.d. p. 159.

"The Young Della Robbia—A Christmas Story," *Christian Science Monitor* December 22,1938, p. 8.

"Christmas Eve, *The Animal Pictorial,* (December, 1938). 3-5.

"The Young Hans Christian Andersen," in *The Shining Tree and Other Christmas Stories.* New York: Alfred A. Knopf, 1940. pp. 77-89.

"Star of Winter," *Yankee,* (December, 1941), 21-22, 32.

"Climb by Moonlight," in Nolen, Barbara (comp.) *Merry Hearts and Bold.* Boston: Heath, 1942. p. 100.

"Eric, Son of Iceland," *Story Parade,* (January, 1942), 16-22.

"Rounding up the Sheep," *American Junior Red Cross News,* (February, 1942), Pt. 1, pp. 143-146. Also in Gruenberg, Sidonie Matsner (comp) *All Kinds of Courage; Stories about Boys and Girls of Yesterday and Today.* Garden City, N.Y.: Doubleday, 1962.pp. 374-383. Also in

Celine, Sister M. *These are our People. Boston: Ginn, 1966.* (Faith and Freedom Basic Readers), p. 406.

"The Marriage Tapestries," *Girls Today,* (September 27, 1942), 3-5. Also in Hazeltine, Alice I. (comp.) *Stories of Love.* New York: Lothrop, Lee & Shepard, 1951. pp. 219-225.

"The Wonder Child," *Child Life,* (May, 1944), 12-14, 36.

"One Heart Inspired with Giving Kindles Christmas Joy for all," *New Hampshire Troubadour,,* (December, 1944), 10-13.

"Once in a Year," *Story Parade,* (December, 1944), 5-12.

"The Village That Changed its Name," *Child Life,* (August, 1946), 10-12.

"Two Boys With a Camera," *Boys Today,* (November 10, 1946), 1-4, 6.

"The Haste-Me Well Quilt," *American Junior Red Cross News,* (April, 1947) 4-7.

"The Christmas Elf," in *Santa's Footprints and Other Christmas Stories.* New York: Aladdin Books, 1948. pp. 77-88.

"The Friendly Ghost," in Kramar, Nora ed. *Arrow Book of Spooky Stories.* New York: Scholastic Book Services, 1962. p. 35. Also in *Spooks and Spirits and Shadow Shapes.* New York: Aladdin, 1949. pp. 19-36.

"Ragnarok, A Spy Story of Iceland," *World Youth,* (April, 1950) 2-16.

"It happened in Cornwall," *Girls Today,* (April 16, 1950), 3-5.

"When the Bells Rang Again for Christmas," *Christian Science Monitor,* Weekly Magazine Section, December 23, 1950, p. 5.

"The Pigeon that Went to Church on Christmas Eve," *North Dakota Teacher,* (December 1950), 10-11,32. Also in *National Educational Association Journal,* (December, 1947), 624-25. Also in Barrow, Marjorie (comp.) *The Peoples Reader,* Chicago: Peoples Book Club. 1949. Pp 40-44.

"The Missing E," in *Big Meeting and Other Festival Tales;* Illustrated by

Billie Nielson, New York: Aladdin, 1950. Pp 92-102

"Boston strikes a Blow for Freedom," in Weber, Alma B. *Coonskin for a General.* New York, Aladdin Books, 1951, pp. 79-87 (Stories of Great American Cities.)

"Over the Seas to Skye..." *World Youth,* (January, 1951), 22-36.

"This Way to Wonder," *Christian Science Monitor,* February, 13, 1951.

"In Search of a Shepherd," *World Youth,* (December, 1951), 40-47.

"Enshrined in the Heart," in Brentano, E. ed. *The World Lives on; a Treasury of Spiritual Fiction.* New York: Doubleday, 1951, pp. 91-96.

"New England Legend," *World Youth* (December, 1952), 2-6.

"Stencils for a Ballroom." In Russell, David H. *Windows on the World.* Boston: Ginn, 1953, p. 238. (The Ginn Basic Readers)

The Piskey Revelers," in Palmer, Robin. *Fairy Elves; a Dictionary of the little People and Some Old Tales and Verses about them.* New York: Henry Z Walck, 1964. Pp. 31-44.

"Sympathetic Ink," *Yankee* (November, 1969), 194-20

ARTICLES WRITTEN FOR VARIOUS MAGAZINES AND NEWSPAPERS

"Bermuda—A Colorful Heaven; a Vivid Impression of Rest," *Smoker's Companion,* I (August, 1927)

"Charlie Ulrich Spent Ten Years Making this Table," *Chamber Contacts,* (Buffalo, NY), Oct. 5, 1928.

"Home weaving in Switzerland," *The Swiss Monthly (*Oct., 1932), 13-16.

"Kilts Crosses the Channel," *New Canaan Advertiser,* (Boston, MA) May 20, 1934.

"A Christian World Statesman; an Interview with Basil Mathews," *Zion Herald,* (Boston, MA), Nov. 11, 1936, p. 1124.

"Seek the Work that Needs You - - Minnie Blagden," *World Youth*, (Nov. 21, 1936), 9.

"A Florentine Craftsman: Della Robbia," *World Youth,* (Dec. 19. 1936), 1.

"A Young English Poet: Margot Dick," *Horn Book Magazine*, (Jan. 1937), 15-19.

"We say 'No!'," *World Youth,* (Jan. 2, 1937)

"Europe, A Prophecy? Blake, the Prophet," *World Youth,* (Feb. 27, 1937)

"Billy Waters: Afternoon with a Fawn," *Horn Book Magazine,* (March, 1937), 113-115.

"Some English Books of 1936," *Horn Book Magazine,* (March, 1937), 116-121.

"Cotswolds have lure," *New York Times,* April 11, 1937, Section 12, p. 7.

"London prepares for the Coronation," *World Youth,* (April 24, 1937), 8-9.

"A School that Loves Animals," *Process Today - - The Humanitarian and Anti-Vivisection Review*, (April-June, 1937), 91-92.

"A Modern Treasure Based on an Ancient Art - - Poole Pottery," *World Youth*, (Sept. 25, 1937)

"'David', Barrie's Last Play," *Horn Book Magazine*, (Sept., 1937), 296-299.

"George MacDonald," *Horn Book Magazine*, (Jan., 1938), 23-29.

"The Isle of Mist," *Horn Book Magazine*, (May, 1938), 150-52.

"Juliana Horatia Ewing," *The Junior Bookshelf*, (July, 1938), 183-186.

"Craftsman of Florence," *The Target*, (April 1, 1939), 8.

"Photographic Illustrations in Books for Children," *The Junior Bookshelf*, (May, 1939), 128-132.

"An Interview with the Author of 'A Testament of Youth'," *World Youth*, May 9, 1939), 9.

"Children's Toys in Iceland," *Horn Book Magazine*, (Jan.-Feb., 1941), 52-55.

"Eating in Iceland," *American Cookery*, (Nov. 1941), 178, 202.

"In Which a Home is Found," *New Hampshire Troubadour*, (Feb. 1942), 7-12.

"Saving Time," *Yankee*, (March, 1942)

"One Small Candle," *Yankee*, (April, 1942), Verso of cover.

"Remember Pearl Harbor," *Yankee*, (May, 1942), Inside back cover.

"Must We Hate?" *Yankee*, (June, 1942), Inside front cover.

"Harvests," *Yankee*, (Nov. 1942), 3.

"How I Began to Write," *Young Wings*, (May, 1943), 12-13, 18.

"Of No Value," *Yankee*, (July, 1943), 43-44, 50, 52-54.

"We Found Patterns on our Walls!" *American Home Journal*, (Oct. 1943), 30-32.

"Susie's Philosophy of Life," *Four Star Final*, (Jan., 1945), 2.

"The Background for *Nearby,*" *Four Star Final,* (Jan., 1947), 6.

"These Things Have Taught Me," *The English Leaflet,* (June, 1946), 88-94.

"The Story of *'Nearby',*" *The Peoples' Choice,* No. 3, 1947, 10-11.

"The Spoken Language in America," *The English Leaflet,* (Dec., 1948), 131-133, 134.

"Beloved Bondage," *The Peoples' Choice,* No. 4, 1949.

"Enys Tregarthen, 1851-1923," *Horn Book Magazine,* (May, 1949). 231-38.

"Portrait of an Artist," *Horn Book Magazine,* (March, 1950), 133-43.

"A Book Comes into Being," *New Hampshire Troubadour,* (August, 1950), 4-6.

"Elizabeth Yates," *New York Herald Tribune Book Review,* Oct. 8, 1950.

"Keep Your Eye on the Rainbow," *Writer,* (May, 1951), 145-48.

"Climbing Some Mountain in the Mind," *Horn Book Magazine,* (July, 1951) 268-278 Newbery Award Acceptance speech.

"Reading to Meet the Challenge of our Day," *National Parent-Teacher,* (Nov. 1951), 24-26.

"Links with the Past," *Christian Herald,* (Nov., 1951), 59,68, 86-87.

"Ten Minutes a Day," *Chicago Schools Journal,* (Jan.-Feb., 1952), 99-101.

"What Shall We Tell Our Children about Death?" *National Parent-Teacher,* (Feb, 1952), 22-24.

"Interview of Mrs. Edward MacDowell," *Peterborough Transcript,* August, 1952, pp. 1,5. Also in *Boston Daily Globe,* August 12, 1952, pp. 1,5.

"Writers' Compass," *Library Journal,* (Oct. 1, 1952), 1567-73.

"Everyman's Quest," *Wilson Library Bulletin,* (Oct., 19540, 151-54.

"Required Reading..." *New Hampshire Profiles,* (Dec., 1955), 17-19.

"Kindling the Creative Spark," *National Parent-Teacher,* (Feb. 1956), 22-24.

"Books are a Bridge," *Library Journal,* (Dec., 1954), 2808-11. Also in *New Hampshire Public Library Bulletin,* (March, 1956), 1-5.

"One Door - - Or Two," *The Michigan Librarian,* (Dec., 1956), 34-36.

"Portraits on Pages," *Writer,* (Feb. 1958), 8-10.

"Writers' Conferences," *Writer,* (April, 1958), 8-10.

"Forward," to Edward Corydon Foote, *With Sherman to the Sea; A Drummer's Story of the Civil War;* as related to Olive Deane Hormel; with a forward by Elizabeth Yates. New York: Day, 1960.

"Writers' Conferences: Viewfinders," *Horn Book Magazine,* (June, 1960), 240-42.

"New Dedication," *Writer,* (Oct. 1960), 17.

"The Mission of the Writer," *The Christian Writer,* (Oct.- Dec., 1960)

"The Things of the Heart," *Baptist Leader,* (Dec., 1960), 12 -13.

"The New England States," *Book of Knowledge,* New York: Grolier, 1962. pp. 6036-41.

"Rich Remembering," *North Country Libraries,* (July, 1961), 1-5.

"Lovely…and of Good Report," *Horn Book Magazine,* (Oct., 1961), 411.

"The Vision Manifest," *Aurora College, A Dedication Record, The Charles B. Phillips Library.* Aurora, Illinois; Aurora College, 1962, pp. 21-25.

"Rewards of Persistence," *Writer,* (Jan., 1963), 19-20.

"Please Answer This…" *Horn Book Magazine,* (April, 1963), 162-64.

"Where is Adventure? *California Librarian,* (Jan., 1964), 33-38.

"Where do you stand?" *Friends Journal,* (Sept., 15, 1965), 453.

"The Glorious Sound;" From the Book *Up the Golden Stair,* by Elizabeth Yates, 1966, E. P. Dutton & Co.

"Helping Children Write," *Childhood Education,* (Dec., 1966), 225.

"All Plus One," *The Watchman Examiner,* (Dec. 15, 1966), 776-78.

"A Writer's Viewpoint on Creativity," *First Seminar on Productive Thinking in Education; Creativity Project.* Saint Paul, Minnesota: Macalester College, 1966. pp. 23-30.

"Birth of a Book," *Yankee,* (March, 1967), 74-75.

"Why did You End Your Story That Way?" *Horn Book Magazine,* (Dec., 1967), 709-14.

"May Sarton," *North Country Libraries,* (March-April, 1969), 16-18.

"Journal of a Woodland Pond" *Forest Notes,* (Winter, 1979-70), 14-15.

"Edward Connery Lathem," *North Country Libraries,* (Sept.-Oct., 1969) 13-17.

"A Unique Sense of Communication," *Horn Book Magazine,* (Oct., 1969), 558-60.

"The Day the Library Closed its Doors," *American Libraries,* (Feb., 1970), 179-80.

"Simple - Simple before God," *Friends Journal,* June 1/15, 1972. (Copy of tear sheet).

"Dog with a Mission," *Good Housekeeping (*April, 1973, 80-81, 84, 86.

"Grandmother's House" Photos by L. Hornstraw. *New Hampshire Echoes* (Nov.- Dec., 1973) 17-21.

"Curtain going up!" Photos curtesy of Sally Stearns Brown. *New Hampshire Echoes,* (Aug. 1974) 56-59.

"The Hostler," Sketches by Nora Unwin, *New Hampshire Profiles,* (Dec., 1974.) 18, 46-47.

"The Legacy" Sketch by Nora Unwin, *New Hampshire Profiles,* (Nov., 1975) 15,45-46.

"Skeezer: the Dog who healed" excerpt from *Skeezer: Dog with a Mission, Reader's Digest,* (Dec. 1975) 241-260.

"Conservation Profile: Lawrence W. Rathbun," *Forest Notes*, 75th Anniversary Double Issue (Fall/Winter, 1976) 33-35.

"Warp and Woof, a talk given on the occasion of the Silver Jubilee of the William Allen White Award," *Library School Review,* Emporia Kansas, 75th Anniversary Issue, 1978.

"Do we Have to Know Everything? *Franklin Pierce Studies in Literature,* 1981, pp. 1-10.

"Letter to the Editor," *Peterborough Transcript,* 8 Oct., 1981.

"Shieling: Half a Mile from the Center of Town" *Forest Notes,* (Winter, 1983) 16-17.

"Elizabeth Yates" *Something about the Author, Autobiography Series,* Vol. 6, pp. 279-296. Gale Research, 1988.

"Holding Time Remote: Place Names that contain Memories" *Forest Notes* (Early Winter. 1993) 18-19.

"Facing up to Time," *Writer,* (March, 1998) 5-6.

Reminiscences of Elizabeth Y. McGreal," Past Chair of the Board and Director Emerita. Excerpts from Ribbon Cutting Remarks, September 17, 1998. *New Hampshire Association for the Blind, 1998 Annual Report & McGreal Sight Center Ribbon Cutting.* p.9

"Reflections of Life in Retirement," *Havenwood-Heritage Heights Retirement Community,* Concord, NH 1999. pp. 1-2.

"Poetry as Dictation" *Forest Notes (*spring 2000) 18.

ARTICLES WRITTEN FOR THE CHRISTIAN SCIENCE MONITOR

Most of the following articles, published in *The Christian Science Monitor,* were written by Elizabeth Yates to accompany photographs taken by her husband while traveling in Europe. Some of these are brief sketches.

"Life Among the Swiss Peasants," March 28, 1933, p.11.

"The Swiss Barn Goes to the Hay," May 31. 1933, p. 5.

"Making a Mountaineer," June 1, 1933. p. 8.

"In Medieval Gruyeres," June 14, 1933, p.9

"Irish Holiday," June 19, 1933, p.7.

"A Street in Old Ronda, Spain," June 24, 1933, p. 5

"Salzburg, Austria," July 8, 1933, p. 7.

"Memorabilia in an Old Address Book," August 2, 1933, p.7.

"Sunlight on Iffigensee, Bernese Oberland, Switzerland," August 14, 1933, p. 7.

"Four pence, Please!" August 21, 1933, p. 8.

"A Letter Arrives in Laudau," September 14, 1933, p. 7.

"The Sign of the Grauer Bar Inn at Insbruck Austria," October 10, 1933, p. 7.

"Two Meet," October 17, 1933, p.7.

"The Kapellbrucke: A Fourteenth Century Bridge, in Lucerne, Switzerland, "October 25, 1933, p.7.

"Pizarra, in Southern Spain," November 10, 1933, p. 7.

"Four Bridges Across the Seine," December 18, 1933, p. 7

"A Garden in Spain," January 18, 1934, p. 7.

"Mountaineering as a Sport," March 29, 1934, p.7.

"Life of a Dog: London,' MAY 3, 1934, P. 16.

"A Bibliophile on the Quai St. Michel," May 19, 1934, p. 7.

"A Letter from Skye," June 19, 1934, p.7.

"Kilts in the Social Whirl," June 19, 1934, p. 16.

"The Family—An Influence for Peace," Weekly Magazine Section, September 12, 1934, pp. 5, 13.

"Kin of Aran," December 21, 1934, p. 7.

"Brittain's Challenge to Youth," Weekly Magazine Section, December 26, 1934, p. 10.

"On Naming Dogs," January 9, 1935.

"Kilts in the Mountains," February 8, 1935, p.14.

"Three Days' Bounty," February 19, 1935, p.14.

"Arrangements," March 2, 1935, p. 5.

"Kilts Crosses an Ocean," May 29, 1935.

"Elizabeth Bergner," Weekly Magazine Section, June 12, 1935, p.3, 13.

"A Tuppenny Chair, March 15, 1935.

"Ten O'Clock," June 10, 1935, p.9.

"The Charm of it all," July 9, 1935, p. 14.

"What is Finger Painting," Weekly Magazine Section, August 14, 1935, pp. 8-9, 12.

"Kilts discovers New York," August 28, 1935.

"Labor Emeritus," Weekly Magazine Section, October 9, 1935, p.7.

"In the Bonds of Radio," Weekly Magazine Section, December 18, 1935, pp. 4, 14.

"Out Upon Comparisons!" February 5, 1936, p.9.

"The Mounts Come to London," February 27, 1936, P. 7.

"Kilts Widens His Circle," April 9, 1936, p.18.

"The Little Fawn, by Billie Waters," May 19, 1936. p. 9.

"They live by the Turn of the Tide," July 28, 1936, p. 14.

"A Scene in Cotswolds, at Chedworth," September 28, 1936, p. 9.

"The Village Nobody Knows," October 9, 1936, p. 9

"A Week in Another World," November 27, 1936, p.9.

"Kilts Answers a Question," November 28, 1936, p. 16.

"Golden Key," January 9, 1937, p. 9.

"A Man in the News," January 16, 1937, p. 4.

"Kilts - - Return of the Native," January 19, 1937, p. 16.

"Tile Makers Turn to Pottery," January 23, 1937, p. 7.

"Ideology," Weekly Magazine Section, March 17, 1937, p. 7.

"Coach and Three," March 25, 1937, p. 18.

"Masks," June 23, 1937, p. 7.

"A Prisoner in Edwardes Square," October 22, 1937, p. 11.

"A Helping Hand in Juvenilia," Weekly Magazine Section,
     January 26, 1938, pp. 8-9.

"Men of the Trees," June 8, 1938, p. 6.

"Sun and Shade in Skye," January 24, 1939, p. 9.

"Parcels in the Post," April 27, 1939, p. 11.

"The Peaceable Kingdom," December 4, 1939, p. 10.

"The Heart of London," January 29, 1940, p. 8.

"Iceland: Democracy's Farthest North," Weekly Magazine Section,
     March 9, 1940, pp. 118-19.

"Night on a Summit," September 5, 1940, p. 10.

"Through the Doorway of King Arthur's Castle," October 24, 1940,
     p. 12.

"St. George and St. Michael," December 7, 1940, p. 18.

"An Icelandic Pony; A Linoleum Print by Nora S. Unwin," May 19, 1941, p. 10.

"In which a Home is Found," August 15, 1941.

"Rainbow on a Shelf," November 27, 1941, p. 10.

"Works of Art," January 16, 1942, p. 12.

"We Prune our Apple Trees," April 30, 1942, p. 8.

"The Pony Transport of Iceland," July 22, 1942, p. 8.

"Have you read it?" September 9, 1942, p. 8.

"And Have You Read This?" December 11, 1942, p. 8.

"Reykjavik Harbor, Iceland, With Mount Esja Looming in the Background," March 27, 1943, p. 8.

"Across the Forest Floor,' December 28, 1943, p. 6.

"Thelma Brackett Makes Library Serve as Center for Interest of the Entire Community," December 28, 1943, p. 9.

"Husband and Family - - Then Dogs are Constance Winant's Interest," February 25, 1944, p. 9.

"New Hampshire League Finds Good Markets for Many Home Craftsmen," June 20, 1944, p. 8.

"Mrs. Thorsen Finds Weaving Rewarding," May 1, 1945, p. 12A.

"Sweet of the Year," April 17, 1947, P. 10.

"Two Hours of a Misty Morning," May 27, 1949, p. 8.

"Where Trees Love to Grow," November 10, 1950. p. 8

"Call of the Wild Spurs U.S. Trail Riders," March 8, 1951, p. 13.

"Sound of Muted Joy, Quiet Delight," April 24, 1951, p. 9.

"More than a Book," September 6, 1951, p. 11

"How an Author and an Artist Work Together," November 15, 1951, p. 13.

PUBLISHED PLAYS

Around the Clock, by Elizabeth Yates and Edith E. Clements, London: James B. Pinker & Son, n.d...10 p.

The Beetle's Ball, by Elizabeth Yates and Edith E. Clements, London: James B. Pinker & Son, n.d...24p.

UNPUBLISHED PLAYS

"After the Wedding," typescript carbon, 12 *l.*

"The Cuckoo Clock," typescript carbon, 32 *l.*

"A Fantasy on Elizabeth Barrett Browning's 'A Musical Instrument,'" typescript carbon, 6 *l.*

"Four Seasons' House," typescript, 30 *l.*

"The Golden Key," typescript, 35 *l.*

"May Magic," typescript carbon 11 *l.*

"Secrets in the Woods," typescript, 35 *l.*

"Sacred to the Memory; Scenes from the Life of Amos Fortune"

PUBLISHED POEMS

"After Parting," *New York Herald Tribune,* July 5, 1927.

"Coast of Maine Portrait," *Town Tidings,* July 1929.

"The Grasshopper," from the Beetle's Ball, London: James B. Pinker & Son,

"Little Green Snake," from: *The Beetle's Ball,* London: James B. Pinker & Son, n.d.

"A New Song," *Horn Book Magazine,* (November-December, 1938), 388-90.

"The Holly Speaks," *Christian Science Monitor,* December 28, 1939, p. 9.

"Jack in the Pulpit," *Christian Science Monitor,* (Taken from clipping.)

"To Dogwood," *Christian Science Monitor (*Taken from clipping)

'Open the door, a Gathering of Poems and Prose pieces." Hopkinton NH: Antiquarian Society, 1999.

"Elizabeth sees with her heart. Then she brings us to see what she sees, to know what she's been given to know, 'announced in these collected poems" Mary Lyn Ray

UNPUBLISHED TALKS

1. "Inside Iceland," (1940) typescript, 12 leaves

2. "Milestones in Reading," (1943) typescript, 11 leaves

3. "Variations on a Chinese Proverb," (Nov. 13, 1944) holograph (pencil)
   7 leaves.

4. Talk at Public Library, Dover, NH (May, 1946) Typescript with one
   holograph page, 10 leaves.

5. Talk at Teachers' College, Keene, New Hampshire (November, 1946)
   typescript, 6 leaves (both sides)

6. "Three Magical Things," (presented on several occasions, 1952-)

7. Talk given at Writers' Conference, University of Indiana (1954)
   typescript, 23 leaves.

8. Talk given at Elliot Community Hospital School of Nursing Capping
   Exercises, (March 9, 1954) typescript, 3 leaves.

9. "The Story in You," (1959?) typescript, 12 leaves.

10. "The Writer's Invisible Tools," (1961) mimeo, 4p.

11. Talk given at Elliot Community Hospital School of Nursing Graduation,
    (1962) typescript 6 leaves.

12. "The Star in Man," (1962?) mimeo, 5p.

13. "Besides Talent, What Else?" (1963) mimeo, 4p.

14. "Not for Publication," (1964) mimeo, 10p.

BIBLIOGRAPHY OF REFERENCES TO
ELIZABETH YATES
ARRANGED IN CHRONOLOGICAL ORDER
BOOKS PERIODICALS AND NEWSPAPERS

Arndt, Jessie Ash," Elizabeth Yates McGreal keeps her time happily in hand," *Christian Science Monitor,* 20 Aug. 1934:10A.

"Some Authors and Artists," *Story Parade,* Oct. 1941: 14.

"Elizabeth Yates Requested to be Patron Author at Keene Teachers' College," *Keene College Kronicle*, 1944: 56.

"Miss Elizabeth Yates at Keene Teachers College," *Keene Evening Sentinel,* 17 April. 1945.

Brackett, Thelma, "Elizabeth Yates," *The Peoples Choice,* 4,3 1947

"Dedicates Book to Keene Women," *Keene Evening Sentinel* 6 Jan. 1947

"Peterborough Author's Book gets Recognition," *Keene Evening Sentinel* 16 Jan. 1947

"Author to Visit Parents," *Buffalo Evening News*, 25 Jan.: 1947

"Miss Yates - An American Miss Goudge," *Chicago Tribune,* 26 Jan. 1947

"People's Book Club Picks *'Nearby'* as Book-of-the-Month," *Peterborough Transcript* 6 Feb. 1947.

"Meet Elizabeth Yates, Authoress, Who Writes About New Hampshire," *New Hampshire Sunday News* 2 March, 1947.

"Elizabeth Yates Named…Woman of the Week," *Peterborough Transcript* 20 Mar. 1947.

Unwin, Nora, "The Joy of Christmas," *Four Star Final,* Fall, 1947: 7

Cimino, M., "Elizabeth Yates," *Wilson Library Bulletin,* Feb. 1948: 422

Arnold, Alison "Women's City Club Entertains Authors at Annual Luncheon" *Boston Herald,* 17 Nov. 1948.

Bond, Alice Dixon, "Elizabeth Yates, Generosity Springs from Serene Spirit," *Boston Sunday Herald,* 12 Dec. 1948.

"Author Addresses Sharon Art Group," *Keene Evening Sentinel* 15 Dec. 1948.

Bangs, Lucille V., "A Well Known Authoress Visits Manchester," *New Hampshire Sunday News,* 30 Jan. 1948.

Worden, Helen, "To the Glory of Amos Fortune," *Collier's* 7 Jan. 1950: 39.

"3 Awards given at Children's Book Festival," *New York Herald Tribune,* 5 May, 1950.

"Mrs. McGreal's Book on Amos Fortune Wins Prize" *The Peterborough Transcript* 11 May, 1950: 1,7.

"UNH Writer's Conference to Offer Prominent Staff," *Morning Union Leader,* 20 June, 1950: 2.

"Author to Autograph Books Here Friday," *Keene Evening Sentinel* 20 July 1950.

"Mrs. McGreal's Amos Fortune Lecture," *Jaffrey Recorder,* 21 July, 1950.

"Important Authors of the Fall, Speaking for Themselves," New *York Herald Tribune Book Review,* 8 Oct. 1950: 2.

Chapin, R. "Miss Yates on the Novel's Goal," *Christian Science Monitor,* 28 Oct. 1950:14.

Morrison, Nyleen "With New Hampshire Woman," *Concord Monitor,* 9 Nov. 1950.

"Newbery Award, 1950," *Top of the News,* March 1951: 14.

"Newbery and Caldecott Awards" Horn *Book Magazine,* March-April, 1951: 66

"Awards to Katherine Milhous and Elizabeth Yates, *"New York Times,* 6 March, 1951: 25.

"Elizabeth Yates Honored," *Buffalo Courier Express,* 7 March, 1951.

"Amos Fortune Book Tops Poll," *Peterborough Express,* 8 March, 1951: 1.

"Elizabeth Yates and Katherine Milhous win Newbury and Caldecott Medals" *Publishers' Weekly,* 10 March, 1951: 1254-57.

"New Hampshire Writer Receives Signal Honor," *Manchester Union Leader 16 March, 1951.*

Bragdon, L.J. "Newbery to Elizabeth Yates," *Library Journal'* 1Apr. 1951: 576.

McGreal, William, "Elizabeth Yates," *Horn Book Magazine,* July,1951: 262-67.

Elizabeth Yates, "Climbing Some Mountain in the Mind," *Horn Book Magazine,* (July-Aug., 1951): 268-78

Thorp, H. Arlene, "The Newbery-Caldecott Dinner" *News Letter (New Hampshire Library Association)* (Oct., 1951): 4-5

"Library Gets Manuscript of Yates Book," *Buffalo Courier-Express,* 16 Dec. 1951:30-d

Yates, Elizabeth, "And then I Knew I Wanted to Write," *Writing Books for Boys and Girls, Ed. By Helen Ferris, Garden City N.Y. The Junior Literary Guild,* Doubleday, 1952.

Peters, Mary, "The Newbery-Caldecott Awards; the Effect on Children's Literature," *Chicago Schools Journal,* Jan.-Feb. 1952: 101.

MacCampbell, James C.., "The Work of Elizabeth Yates," *Elementary English* Nov., 1952: 381-89.

Mikkanen, Mildred, "Want to Write? - Ten Established Authors, at New Hampshire University Conference., Tell us the Secrets of What Makes a Writer Click," *Worcester Sunday Telegram,* 9 Nov. 1952: 3.

"William Allen White Children's Book Award," *Top of the News* May, 1953: 24.

"Children's First Choice," *Kansas Library Bulletin,* June - Sept. 1953: 3—4.

"Former Buffalonian Tells Tender Tale in Day of Stark Realism," *Buffalo Courier,* 4 Oct. 1953: 43C.

"Children Should have Love for Books, Says Miss Elizabeth Yates," *The Emporia Gazette,* 8 Oct. 1953: 1.

"Elizabeth Yates Says Books Help Set Ideals for Children," *The Hays Daily News,* 11 Oct. 1953: 1

O'Connor, Lois, "Writer for Children says, 'Put Wonder into Words' for Them," *Ithaca Journal* 17 Oct. 1953.

Reilly, Alice, "Notes and Comments," *Kansas Library Bulletin,* Dec., 1953: 9-12.

"Our First Meeting," *The Bulletin of the Boston Authors Club,* Dec., 1953: 3.

"Doing a Good Turn," *Peterborough Transcript,* 14 Nov., 1954.

"Elizabeth and William," *San Francisco Progress,* 17 Aug., 1955:16.

"'Rainbow Round the World' Wins Jane Addams Medal for Mrs. McGreal," *Peterborough Transcript,* 8 Sept. 1955.

"Cleveland Plays Host to Authors, Artists, Celebrities," *Cleveland Press,* 1 Nov. 1955: 13., 20.

'Miss Yates Receives Addams Award," *The Ithaca Journal,* 21 Nov. 1955.

Mahoney, Helen H., "New Hampshire Woman Author 'relaxes' on Pack Trips, *The Boston Sunday Globe,* 12 Nov., 1956: 7 A.

Smith, H. Katherine, "Mrs. McGreal's Books Show Strong NY Flavor," *Buffalo Courier Express,* 17 Nov. 1957.

"Elizabeth Yates at Aurora College: Lectures on Two Recent Biographies," *The Aurora Borealis,* April, 1959.

Glimmer, Josephine D., "Prayers from Many Lands," *Worcester Sunday Telegram Feature Parade,* 7 May, 1959: 21-22.

Stix, Harriet, "Writer Needed a Push to Talk about Herself," *New York Herald Tribune,* 14 July. 1960:19.

Kendle, Kate, "Peterborough Author Autographs New Book," *Keene Evening Sentinel* 15 July, 1960: 2

"The McGreals' Great Life Story," *Laconia Evening Citizen,* 20 July, 1960.

Greenwood, Walter B. "Miss Yates Etches Warm Simple Novel in Rustic Setting." *Buffalo Evening News,* 6 Jan., 1962.

Hebert, Ernest, "Creative Writers, Scholars join for Conference at b., 'Miss Yates Etches Warm, Simple Novel in Rustic Setting.' *Buffalo Evening News,* 6 Jan. 1962.

Hipple, Glen, "Elizabeth Yates' Novel Started with Idea from 1 Paragraph Story." *Keene Evening Sentinel,* 6 Jan. 1962: 1.

Stuart, Reece, "To Warm a Reader's Heart," *Des Moines Sunday Register* 28 Jan. 1962: 17G.

"National Library Week - April 9 to 14," *New Hampshire Town Crier,* 5 Apr., 1962: 4-5,9.

"Elizabeth Yates Will Present Second Advent Service Program," *Daily Item,* Wakefield MA. 7 Dec. 1962.

"How a Book is Born," *The Brattleboro Daily Reformer,* 27 Apr., 1963: 8.

"Blind Association Annual Held." *Concord Daily Monitor,* 3 June, 1964.

Fox, Kay," Elizabeth Yates Data Surveyed by Librarian," *Keene Evening Sentinel,* 22 Oct. 1964: 16.

Hewitt, Ruth, "Noted Writer Plans Classes at College," *Aurora Beacon News,* 14 Nov. 1964, Supplement: 3.

"Author Says Early Reading Pays off," *Aurora Beacon News,* 18 Nov. 1964.

Friedland, John, "Author Stresses Imagination," *Aurora Borealis* 23 Nov., 1964:1

"Book Attributed to Aurora Visit," *Aurora Beacon News,* 25 Nov., 1964.

"Elizabeth Yates Honored," *North Country Libraries,* Nov-Dec., 1964: 20.

"The Wilder Nominees…Elizabeth Yates-'A Gentle Tranquil Faith'" *Top of the News,* Jan., 1965: 128-30.

Campbell, M.K., "Elizabeth Yates," *North Country Libraries,* Jan. 1965: 11—13.

Painter, Helen W. "Elizabeth Yates: Artist With Words," *Elementary English,* Oct. 1965: 617-28.

"The Inside Story of the Sussex Country Library," *Boston Sunday Herald,* 17 Oct. 1965.

"Writer Elizabeth Yates Key Speaker at Ninth Reading Conference," 29 Sept., 1966.

Brady, Karon, "Buffalo Born Author Keeps Abreast of the Times by Staying Old-Fashioned," *Buffalo Evening News,* 29 Oct. 1966.

"Creative Reading Goes Beyond Mere Understanding and Literal Interpretation; Leads to Conclusion or Solves Problem," *Massena, N.Y. Observer,* 1 Nov. 1966.

"A Unique Contribution by Elizabeth Yates," *New Hampshire Sunday News,* 6 Nov. 1966.

"Miss Yates, Lent Speaker," *Brattleboro Daily Reformer,* 9 Mar. 1967: 3

Wolfe, Christine, "Kids Love Her Books!" *Record American,* (Boston Mass) 9 June, 1969: 24.

Vining, Elizabeth Gray, "A Quaker Profile: Elizabeth Yates McGreal," *Friends Journal,* 15 Oct. 1969: 580-81.

Woodbury, George, "A Deeply Moving Story by Peterborough Writer," *New Hampshire Sunday News,* 26 Oct. 1969.

Robinson, Ann," Peterborough Author Speaker for Local DAR's Anniversary," *Keene Evening Sentinel,* 3 Oct. 1971: 3.

Cohn, Richard, "Temple Tale TV-Born," *The Peterborough Transcript,* 6 Jan. 1972: 1,4.

Jennings, Maureen, "Elizabeth Yates succeeding on Writing Talent, not Genius," *Keene Evening Sentinel,* 22 Apr. 1972: 1-2.

"In Search of Sarah Whitcher," [the story of a Miracle and how a distinguished Author journeyed back into New Hampshire's Past to Retell it] *New Hampshire Echoes,* Sept., 1972: 30-33.

"Authors Honored for New Book," *Daily Eagle,* (Claremont, N.H.) 21 Oct., 1974: 5.

"Yates' New Book Hailed as Bicentennial Aid," *The Argus-Champion* (Newport, N.H.) 30 Oct. 1974: 16.

"'We the People' Sells Out. Crowd Attends Area's First Bicentennial Event," *The Ledger,* 31 Oct. 1974: 3

Callahan, Jim, "Recent Work Illustrates talents—Area Author McGreal Reveals Patience and Work Involved in Writing Profession." *The Ledger,* 17 Dec., 1975, Sec. 3: 1, 11.

Johnson, Erna, "'A Quiet Goodness of Spirit' Prolific Writer Elizabeth Yates Shares Some of Her Methods," Milford N.H. *Cabinet and Wilton Journal,* 27 Apr., 1978: 14.

"Historical Society will hear Author," *Evening Citizen* (Laconia, N.H.) 21 July, 1978.

"Newbery Award Winner Elizabeth Yates to begin Lecture Series of 'Values Week'" *The Chautauguay Daily,* 24 July 1978: 1.

"Author at White Pines," *Nashua Telegraph,* 21 Dec. 1978.

"Our Board of Directors - Who are they?" *New Hampshire Association for the Blind,* 22 Aug., 1979.

Rich, Elaine Sommers, "Thinking with—A True Pioneer Story" *Mennonite Weekly Review,* 22 Nov. 1979.

"Home Grown Literature," *Leisure,* 28 Feb., 1980:1,8-10.

"Shieling Forest Given to NH." *The Peterborough Transcript,* 27 March, 1980.

"Shieling Forest Will Teach Wood Growers," *The Peterborough Transcript* 22 Aug. 1980.

"Mrs. McGreal Citizen of Year" *The Peterborough Transcript,* 26 Nov. 1980: 1.

Carnog, Mary, "Elizabeth Yates: Optimist," The *Monadnock Ledger, 10* Dec. 1980: 3

"Chamber Honors Citizen of Year," *The Monadnock Ledger,* 10 Dec. 1980: 3

Allen, Mary E., "Elizabeth Yates tells about Sarah Whitcher," *The Record Citizen,* (Plymouth, N.H.) 13 May 1981.

Herbert, Ernest, "Creative Writers, Scholars join for Conference at Franklin Pierce," *The Keene Sentinel,* 10 Oct. 1981; 5.

Graves, Pat, "Elizabeth Yates: Peterborough Author," *Leisure,* 5 Nov. 1981: 11.

Allen, Mary E., "Elizabeth Yates' latest book." *The Record Citizen,* (Plymouth, N.H.) 2 Dec. 1981.

"Shieling Forest Opens with Sunday Trail Walk," *Monadnock Ledger,* 22 Sept. 1982: 2.

Wolseley, Roland E., "The Spiritual Rewards of Writing," *Interlitt Publishing Strategy,* March 1983; 22-23.

McGoldrick, Linda C., "Elizabeth Yates, "New *Hampshire Times,* 24 Mar. 1984: 17-19.

"The McGreal Sight Center," *The New Hampshire Association for the Blind,* Special Issue - Dedication. 15 June 1985.

Paiste, Dennis "Helpers of Blind Dedicate Building to Bill McGreal." *Concord Monitor,* 15 June, 1985.

"Centennial Gift" *Granite State Libraries (*Concord N.H.) Aug.-Sept.1989: 9

Sumner, Deborah, "Growing old is just growing up, so says Peterborough author Elizabeth McGreal," *Keene Sentinel Magazine, Observer* 25-31 Aug. 1990: 6-8.

"The William and Elizabeth Yates McGreal Society for the Endowment of the New Hampshire Association for the Blind." *The New Hampshire Association for the Blind Newsletter,* September, 1992.

Hamm, Christine, "An Author Shares Her Secrets," *Concord Monitor* 8 Apr. 1993: B1, B10.

Rebecca Rule," A Writer, from her teens to her 90s" *Concord Monitor,* Sept. 15, 1996: I, 3-4.

Barnes, Jack, "Dear Diary: 'I want to be a Writer'" *New Hampshire Sunday News,* 23 Feb., 1997.

"Lady of Grace, Elizabeth Yates McGreal," *Havenwood-Heritage Heights* (Concord, N.H.) 1999: 1.

Hendryx, Nancy, "Kindred Spirits" *Concord Monitor,* 20 Oct. 1999.

Eklund, Jane, "Elizabeth Yates McGreal dies in Concord." *Monadnock Ledger,* Peterborough, N.H., Aug. 2, 2001: 1, 8.

"Elizabeth Yates McGreal" (Obituary) *Monadnock Ledger,* 2 Aug. 2001: 4.

"Remembering McGreal; Author was productive member of Community." *Monadnock Ledger (*Opinion) 2 Aug., 2001: 10.

"Elizabeth Yates McGreal, Newbery Award winner"; *The Union Leader:* (Obituaries) Aug. 2, 2001: A-6.

Graham, Jim: "Yates took her time to visit Fortune": *The Sunday Telegraph* (Nashua, N.H.) 5 Aug., 2001: G-7.

Long, Tom; "Elizabeth Yates McGreal, wrote children's classic; 95" *The Boston Globe,* (Obituaries) 5 Aug. 2001,

STANDARD BIOGRAPHICAL COLLECTIONS

Current Biography. Who's News and Why, 1948. New York: Wilson 1949: 659-98.

Contemporary Authors: A biobibliographical Guide to Current Authors and Their Works. Vols 1-4. Gale Research, 1967: 1032-33.

Kunitz, Stanley Jasspon and Haycraft, Howard (eds) *Junior Book of Authors,* 2d ed. revised. New York: Wilson, 1951: 303-305.

Kunitz, Stanley Jasspon. (ed.) *Twentieth Century Authors.* 1st supplement. New York: Wilson, 1955: 1113-14.

Major Authors and Illustrators for Children and Young Adults; a selection of Sketches from Something about the Author: (edited by) Laurie Collier and Joyce Nakamura. Gale Research, 1993: 2519-22.

The National Cyclopaedia of American Biography. Volume H. New York: White 1892-1965: 234-35.

"Newbery Medal Books," 1922-1955, *The Horn Book Inc.* 1955: 353-371.

Twentieth-Century Children's Writers, Editor: D.L. Kirkpatrick. New York: St. Martin's Press, 1978: 1373-77.

Something About the Author, autobiography Series, Gale Research, 1988; Vol. 6. pp. 279-296.

Something About the Author; facts and pictures about authors and illustrators of books for Young People; edited by Donna Olendorf. Gale Research, 1992: 236-8 bibl. illus. pors.

Ward, Martha E. and Marquardt, D.A. *Authors for Young People.* New York: Scarecrow, 1964: 280-281.

Warfel, Harry Redcay. *American Novelists of Today.* New York: American Book Co., 1951: 471.

*Who's Who in America...*Vol. 35, 1968-1969. Chicago: Marquis,
   1968: 2412.

Who's Who of American Women. 5th ed. Chicago: Marquis, 1967: 1354.

World Authors 1900-1950; editors, Martin Seymour-Smith and Andrew
   Kimmens, W. H. Wilson: 1996: 2965-7.

A TIME TO REMEMBER

ELIZABETH YATES McGREAL

December 6, 1905 - July 29, 2001

HAVENWOOD-HERITAGE HEIGHTS

Elizabeth requested that there be "no memorial service" and "no eulogy after she died. She wanted only a time for friends to gather and share memories, to comfort each other. So, after the manner of Friends, the seating in this room and the structure of this time will be for people to face each other, listen, remember, reflect, and share as the Spirit moves. It is not out of disrespect that we do not name the many achievements and accolades of Elizabeth's life, but a deep respect for her wishes that this time is fashioned in this way.

So welcome, friend, to this time and this place
Where both the silence and the sharing
May be a consolation
And an honoring of Elizabeth

Following this time, everyone is invited to have light refreshments and to continue the conversation in the Coffee Shop and Corridor areas.

Peterborough
February 9, 1984

Dear Sister Margaret,

You could not guess what a help you are to me right now!

Perhaps I told you that MY DIARY, MY WORLD is being followed this spring (May 1st) by MY WIDENING WORLD which takes me up to and through 1929, when my life was in London and Bill and I were married.

Now, quite unbelievably, the publishers want me to go on to 1951 – this will be almost entirely concerned with writing and the books that came into being during those years. I kept a loose kind of journal then, and I had a series of notebooks, but actual titles, publications, dates had not been kept in many cases and all of these I have found in your complete Bio-Bibliography of me. My work the last few weeks has been made so much easier because of that tremendous and careful research you did. I do thank you very much.

But don't you think you stop too soon?

My warm good wishes to you and my deep appreciation for all you have done for me and are doing for those whom your life touches.

Yours,

Elizabeth Y. W.

ABOUT THE AUTHOR

Sister Margaret Trudell is a sister of the Congregation of the Presentation of Mary from the Manchester NH Province. While serving the order she first taught in the elementary grades, she then spent thirty-seven years as librarian at Rivier College in Nashua New Hampshire. She dedicated three years to Casa de Esperanza, in Houston, Texas, which is a House of Hope for children in crisis, due to neglect, abuse or the effects of HIV. Through the years, Sister earned a Masters in Education from Rivier College and a Masters in Library Science from Catholic University of America in Washington D.C. Sister is now residing at Presentation of Mary Academy in Hudson, New Hampshire.